For

Andre, Dave, Mike, Richie, Tim
and Coach Dave

# Acknowledgements

Without the undying support of my friends, this book would never have been possible.

To Kimbo: 48 years is a long time, but no one knows me better. You have always been and will always be the conscience of my soul, my oldest and dearest friend, and the shoulder to always cry and laugh on. Together we have been to hell and back. Your brotherhood, love, and loyalty honor me. Smith Street Smashers rule!

To Vinnie: When it was unpopular to befriend me, you opened your heart. You are a true friend and no one is luckier than I to have your telephone number. Your spirit and friendship honor me.

To Rick, Scott, Chris, and Bonnie: We are forever bonded by September 11. I survive because of each of you. You were there when I laughed and cried. You know the feelings, the emotions, and heartache I endure daily, and I yours. Together, we have explored the fine line between laughter and anguish. Each of you, in your own inimitable way, has touched my soul. You are each now, and forever, a part of me, and I thank God for that every day.

To Minna, Kevin, Dave, Tom, Bettina, Joan, Sean, Rich, Bill, Diana, and Marge: Thank you one and all for not only doing your jobs professionally, but also with honor, integrity, and caring. What you each contribute is a Godsend, and the world is a better place because of you.

To Frank, Aileen, Ray, and Debbie: In all of you, soundness of mind, uncompromising principle, and honor abounds. You have all transcended our rapport through your unbending ethics, uncanny sense of what is right and just, and the embodiment of what true friendship is. God has blessed me with your friendship, and I am profoundly gratified by it.

To Pastors Kirschbaum and Taylor: *Est autem fides credere quod non dum vides; cuius fidei merces est videre quod credis.* (Faith is to believe what you do not see, the reward of this faith is to see what you believe.)

To Barry: As of this writing, we are yet to meet, but you wore your heart on your sleeve. Our relationship has blossomed into binding camaraderie, and I am truly fortunate to have you as my friend. Absolutely none of this would have happened without your guidance, caring, and enthusiasm.

# Dedication

*To Mom and Dad – Emory and Marilyn Wright.*

As I get older, I remember the life lessons you've taught me. Through your love and encouragement, you gave me the strength to go on when I was searching the windows of my soul and the essence of my being after September 11, despite being surrounded by death, despair, and degradation. On September 16, 2001, I faced certain death while inside the pile when it started to shake. Only through the faith you taught me, was I able to endure.

Mom, you stayed steadfast in your maternal tenet, especially when our opinions differed. Your telephone calls during the first week after September 11, were the foundation that strengthened my soul, reinforced my resolve, and gave me the capacity to go on. Among upheaval mired by controversy and surrounded by adversity, you were the calm in the eye of the hurricane. A better mom does not exist.

Dad, you taught me countless lessons during the youth of my life. Pop, the things you taught me saved my life on more than one occasion. None more so than on September 16, at Ground Zero when I thought my end was near. You taught me to believe in a spiritual life. You taught me that it was all right to root for the underdog and to stand up for the less fortunate. You taught me it was all right to take on a corrupt establishment and to try and make a difference in someone's life each and every day. You taught me how to love my children unconditionally. You taught me that no matter what, I should be fearless in the face of threat, compassionate in the face of indifference, and faithful in the face of the uninspired. You are my hero.

George "Pop" Wright, Jon's grandfather.

# One

# Tuesday, September 11, 2001

EVERYBODY knows what happened on September 11 — but for me, it was different. All the good and bad parts of being a firefighter rolled into that one day. A day seared forever into my memory.

It started out like a regular day. I woke as usual at about 5 a.m. The sun was rising, the skies were clear, and the temperature was forecast for the upper seventies. I stepped out onto my front porch in South Freeport and left for my morning walk, returning about 6:30 am.

As I said, the day began just like it usually does. My youngest son, Christian, was preparing for school. By trade, I am a home improvement contractor, and I was preparing for the day's work when my telephone rang. My father was calling from his retirement home in North Carolina as he did every day to say hello before I left for work. Dad's a retired contractor whose health, sadly, is failing. I worry about him.

Dad had been a member of the Freeport Fire Department for forty-six years. And he'd followed my grandfather, George Wright, who was a fifty-seven year member. I followed in my father's footsteps, and I've been at it for thirty years. The most memorable times of my life were running with my dad to the firehouse on Church Street when a fire call sounded. The memory always brought a smile to my face. Often he let me get there ahead of him so I could open the bay doors to let the fire trucks out. Countless times my father, grandfather and I sat on construction jobs as I listened

to them tell their fire department war stories. My older
brother Randy was also a firefighter and sometimes, he
listened in too. I was particularly fond of stories about
firemen at the bay house and how they went fishing,
clamming, made clam chowder, ate and then fell asleep until
dawn.

Now my children listen to my stories, and I appreciate
my father and grandfather even more. I hope my boys follow
in my footsteps: Because in spite of the bad things that occur,
and there have been plenty of bad times, working as a
fireman has been the best time of my life. The feeling of
saving a life is indescribable, even humbling. It is truly a
remarkable feeling that I have been fortunate to experience.

Dad knew I had started a job for one of his old
customers, Jack Holly. Jack's an affable man, a likeable sort
whom I respect and admire. I'd met Jack at the Freeport
Recreation Center, and when I told him who my father was,
he asked me to do work on his house, as my father had
twenty-five years earlier. Jack's very involved in the Long
Island Arts Council.

Dad asked about my older son Brendan, who was in his
freshman year at Oneonta State College in upstate New York.
I had dropped him off there just three weeks earlier. That was
particularly emotional because I realized he's an adult now,
no longer the little boy who played PeeWee football. No
longer the kid who ran and jumped into my arms after every
game because he was so happy that he'd played.

Brendan's athletic prowess had continued throughout his
high school years, and constantly made me proud of his
accomplishments, both on and off the athletic field. He is an
extraordinary athlete; which explains why he was named team
captain for the football and lacrosse teams. We could not
have predicted on that fateful fall day that one month later,
during a football game against Hewlett High School,
Brendan's left elbow would be completely dislocated –

intentionally – by one of Hewlett's players.

Brendan would be out for the year and with the playoffs approaching, he was devastated. Inconsolable he writhed in pain on the way to the hospital. It was truly a father's worst nightmare. After they popped his dislocated elbow back in, we left the hospital and for the next three weeks, he worked hard at his physical therapy. On more than one occasion, I watched him endure agonizing pain. It reduced me to tears. I'd always known how compassionate he was, but now I know how tough and competitive he can be. He is my son, and I love him dearly.

In November, exactly three weeks after the injury, Brendan led his team onto the football field at Hofstra Stadium for the first round of the playoffs. When they announced his name, his picture was shown on the huge scoreboard screen and he received a standing ovation. They lost the game, but Brendan received another standing ovation – due mostly to the fact he played the game of his life with only one arm, like Junior Seau in the Super Bowl against San Francisco. The crowd always loves a competitor. His injured arm was locked in a brace to prevent further injury. To me, Brendan epitomizes team play and the competitive spirit. He led his team by example. November 4, 2001 had become the proudest day of my life.

On this morning of September 11, I drove to Bob's Luncheonette to get my traditional morning tea and newspaper. I went to the job, backed into Jack's driveway and opened my morning paper.

The radio was tuned to Z-100 FM. As is their custom, the DJ's played practical jokes on people over the telephone while the audience listened and laughed. This morning they told the woman on the telephone that the cat she was planning to take on the plane with her to Florida could no longer accompany her due to improper seating arrangements.

The woman went berserk towards the people at the radio station until they let on this was indeed a practical joke. Anyone who heard this skit must have laughed as hard as I did. The joke was on her, although I doubt she laughed. I can still hear her saying, "My cat's going," dozens of times. The bit only lasted a few minutes.

While I fingered through the sports pages, the DJ's at made an announcement that a plane had crashed into the World Trade Center.

I said to myself, "These DJ's crossed the line with this practical joke." I didn't think it was funny and was offended by it. I brushed it off as irresponsible or stupid. After all, this was part of the radio station persona.

They kept at it, and I started to sense urgency in their voices. I remembered what my son Brendan had said four weeks earlier, and I jumped out and headed upstairs to Jack's attic.

Brendan had helped me on Jack's job the week before he left for college, and I clearly remember him asking: "Can you see the World Trade Center from the attic?"

"I doubt it," I'd said, but he'd looked anyway.

When he came down he told me, "It's a beautiful sight from so far away." I remembered going up to see for myself, and it truly was majestic.

Now peering out the attic window, looking westward toward New York City, I saw humanity's lowest moment. It was the most terrifying sight I've ever seen. It put the fear of God in me. A straight plume of thick, black smoke drifted unrelentingly from north to south, coming straight from the World Trade Center. Reality set in. Reality hits with a resounding thud, like a hammer between the eyes. A chill came over me, just like it came over the rest of America.

This was no joke. I knew this was something of cataclysmic proportion, worse than any head-on train collision. Worse than anything since Pearl Harbor.

In Freeport, where no buildings are more than five stories tall, a plane into a building would be catastrophic, but we firefighters would be able to deal with it. In New York City, the planes hit on the eighty-seventh and one-hundredth floors. I can't imagine what went through everyone's collective minds.

Immediately, I thought about the initial explosions, and how the people would escape from the upper floors. If they *could* escape from the upper floors.

"Were firefighters already up there?" I wondered. "How did they escape?" I asked nobody in particular.

"What about the people above the crash and explosions? What about the people on the plane?" My mind raced. "What about the people on the floors where the planes hit?"

For the next several days, these thoughts and questions would shroud my mind. They'd keep me uneasy, unable to sleep. To this day, I'm still haunted by the events.

I was coming down from the attic when my cell phone rang. My wife Dorothy said, "Get to a television. An airliner has crashed into the World Trade Center." She added that many had most likely been killed. I told her I'd call her back and immediately responded to my firehouse.

While en route, my fire department pager went off. Fire Com (Nassau County Fire Communications) had put out an urgent call for all fire chiefs to call in. I called the firehouse and got news of the unfolding tragedy. I am a member of Emergency-Rescue Company #9, Freeport Fire Department and duty was calling. Intensely, I listened to the radio reports about the events unfurling. My hands gripped the steering wheel tighter. By the time I arrived at the firehouse, there was sheer panic in the voices of the radio DJ's. I was unnerved.

Others had already assembled at the fire station. The looks on their faces startled me. Inside the station, I looked at the television. I got a debilitating knot in my stomach like none I'd ever felt before. I had to lean on the railing in front of the couch. It had only been about twenty minutes since the first announcement of the tragedy, but it seemed like an eternity already.

We got to the T.V. in time to see the second airliner crash into Tower One. Completely disappear is more like it. Straight into the tower structure itself, an explosion of flame and turmoil. A split-second later, we watched the nose cone of the plane exit the other side of the building at a high rate of speed, simultaneously exploding. It looked like ten floors had blown up.

About forty-five minutes later, we witnessed the collapse of Tower 2 of the World Trade Center, followed fifteen minutes later with the collapse of Tower 1. We were in complete shock.

Within minutes the telephone rang. I answered, and Chief John Wensley informed me that several current and former Freeport Firefighters were among those missing in the collapse. These firefighters were Lt. Timothy Higgins (Hose 2), Ex Captain Richie Muldowney (Engine Company), Firefighter Dave Weiss (Engine Company), Firefighter Mike Kiefer (Engine Company), and Firefighter Andre Fletcher (Hose 5). Several weeks later I found out that my son Christian's Little League coach, Dave Garcia, had also gone missing.

This was now the worst day of my life; four of the six people who'd worked for me in my construction business at one time or another were gone. Later I would look into Christian's eyes and tell him "Coach Dave" had been killed He cried in my lap for hours.

But now our eyes remained glued to the television, and we began wondering aloud if we would be called. We wanted to do something. We wanted to find our brothers. We wanted to be involved. Minutes turned into hours and hours turned into days. We wanted to bring our brothers home, but we waited. Just waited. Helpless. Or rather, unable to help.

Unable to move.

On the first day, we watched the television with resolve for hours on end. Two hours into the ordeal, Excelsior Hook and Ladder Company #1, known to us as Truck Company, was summoned to respond to what was now officially dubbed "Ground Zero". Leading that crew was Lt. Chris Stebner, whose father Kent Stebner, like my father and grandfather, is an ex-captain of Truck Company. That Company has several members who are New York City firefighters, and after pulling some strings, they were called in to assist in the search and rescue effort.

That was the first time I remember a volunteer fire department being called in to assist the FDNY – and this was only the beginning. More volunteer fire departments were being called in. And after two days, it was complete pandemonium. I mean brutal, emotional, gut-wrenching pandemonium.

Volunteer fire departments from all over Nassau and Suffolk Counties had started to respond into Manhattan without being called. The mutual aid system had a thought-provoking breakdown, which led to a complete collapse of the Incident Command System. The Incident Command System is the foundation used on all types of emergencies by both the fire and police departments. I remember thinking, what were the chances we would get into Manhattan to participate in the search and rescue if this system had a complete breakdown?

The answer would come soon enough.


Wednesday, September 12.

I got out of bed and went straight to the firehouse. Captain Bentley was there when I arrived. He told me he'd been ordered by Chief Wensley to put together a list of firefighters willing, if called, to go to Ground Zero.

"I am available immediately," I said, not stopping to think.

Just then, Lt. Frank Tucker walked in. "I'll go," he said matter-of-factly.

I volunteered to call the members one by one and ask. No one refused. Just as I finished making the calls, my cell phone rang. My father – calling to tell me to be careful. "Somehow, I knew you would try to get into Manhattan to participate in the rescue operations."

That day, my sister in-law, Janet, my niece Michelle, and Aunt Carol all called. All three offered the same advice; they told me to be careful. It seems they knew what was to come and knew I would be in the middle of it. Those four phone calls did little to ease my anxiety, but the gestures were heartwarming. My family cared for me.

We were hungry, and I needed to get back to the job and check in with Jack. I volunteered to get lunch on the way back, and off I went.

Back at my job, I met Jack at the front door. He looked me straight in the eye and said, "I don't expect you anytime soon." He understood how serious the situation was and that the events of the last two days took precedent. He made it clear it was okay to go to Manhattan and to put his job on hold. I don't know if he realized how symbolic that was, but I will never forget it.

I returned to the firehouse. Captain Bentley said, "Start preparing the heavy rescue truck. Go over each and every compartment on the truck and all the tools and equipment in them."

He further told me to make certain the Hurst Tool – known as the Jaws of Life – was fully operational, that torches had gas, and the saws had gasoline. Then he added, "Start preparing for the worst."

I asked why, and when he replied, "We're on a heightened state of alert against more terrorist attacks." That

got my undivided attention. I thought to myself, we are at war
– where are my kids?

Brendan was upstate at college and Christian was at Bay
View Avenue School. For now they were safe, but I thought
of them constantly.

The station received numerous faxes about possible
terrorist activity in and around the metropolitan area,
including Freeport. We received one particularly disturbing
fax about terrorists stealing emergency vehicles, most notably
fire department ambulances, driving them to predetermined
targets, and detonating bomb-laden ambulances.

Others included warnings about trains being a suicide
bomber target and the use of biological warfare agents like
Anthrax and Saran gas being released in public places with
large numbers of people. The Long Island Railroad is directly
across the street from Freeport Fire Headquarters, which
made us more alert. We were told to be suspicious of anyone
who appeared of Middle-Eastern descent, and we received
faxes from the F.B.I., Nassau County Police Department, the
Nassau County Fire Marshal's Office, Nassau County Fire
Com, and the Nassau County Office of Emergency
Management.

The first three days after the initial attack were ominous.
In addition to being on heightened alert for more terrorist
activity, we still had to respond to fire and rescue calls. Every
call we went on was met with incredible security, keen
awareness, and an eye towards unwavering observation. I
found myself eyeballing everything I came into contact with.
When I entered a house for a fire or rescue call, I peeked into
the doorway first before entering. Only when I felt it was safe
would I enter. I began observing everything inside homes. I
noticed pictures on walls, items on a kitchen table, and
toiletries in the bathroom. I looked for anything out of the
ordinary – anything that would pique my curiosity and help
thwart these evil murderers. I am a senior firefighter and have

a responsibility to look out for my brother firefighters at all times and in all situations. Thank God I never found anything reportable. I don't know how I would have reacted had I found something.

Thursday, September 13

Day three brought more of the same. We had received word that within a few days a caravan of heavy rescue trucks would be going to downtown Manhattan to light up the area. Lighting was desperately needed because the power in downtown Manhattan was out.

Captain Dave Bentley called on my cell phone and asked, "Are you still willing to go into Manhattan?"

"Yes," I said.

He asked me to meet him to discuss strategy. We met for lunch at the firehouse. When I arrived, my old friend Charlie Naumann was there, sweeping the floor. I think he felt the need to be involved somehow. Charlie had worked for my father many years before in the construction business. He's a gentle man with a big heart and there was nothing he wouldn't do for you if you asked. I am glad he is my friend.

Captain Bentley and I finished lunch, then retreated to the meeting room where we discussed who should go into Manhattan if we were called. I was flattered when he asked my opinion. We traded thoughts for about an hour about who should go and why.

I confided to him that in 1995 I was diagnosed with Post Traumatic Stress Disorder because I never talked about the emotional trauma I endured during my fire service career. I told him I'd spent one year in counseling and said, "It was the best thing to happen to me." It was a learning experience and I was grateful to Dr. O'Ragin for all her help and insight.

I also told him I thought it would be an enormous mistake to take any of the younger firefighters – I felt they'd be more easily scarred for life. We were about to embark on something we'd never experienced before. I felt older, more seasoned firefighters would be his best choice because they are more stable and readily able to handle the emotional problems that were bound to arise. He agreed, and made a list of who to call first. Furthermore, he advised me that I would be the one making the calls when the need arose.

Captain Bentley is a strong, quiet man who always gets the job done. He never has to point a finger or discipline anyone publicly. The weight of the world had been thrown on his shoulders, and I can think of no one else I would rather go to Ground Zero with. He is an easy-going man and one of the best officers I have ever known. In the midst of criticism because of his quiet demeanor, he kept a cool head and always prevailed. It's an honor and privilege to know him.

Within days, I would get to know him even better.

Two

# Freeport Fire Department Hockey Team

WE'D been at Ground Zero for several hours and had yet to
find any survivors. Charlie McEneaney and I were crawling in
and out of holes, moving everything in our way and getting
bumps and bruises all over our bodies.

The concrete chunks, which appeared after the collapses,
were in some cases the sizes of basketballs. The
reinforcement rods inside the concrete forms were a mangled
mess of steel in every direction. When looking up at the
American Express building, a piece of steel that had become
a projectile after the initial crash and explosion was lodged on
a forty-five degree angle through one side of the building and
out another, on about the fiftieth floor. Charlie and I
continued digging until we found a hole.

As I crawled into this particular hole – which was no
bigger than a computer monitor – I shined my hand-light
ahead of me. I saw what appeared to be several pieces of
paper with what I knew must be blood all over it. My heart
raced and pounded. Pounded like the Rolling Stones' Charlie
Watts, beating on trashcans. Beating into my throat. Beating
in my chest and down to my toes. I reached in ahead of
myself and pulled a couple of pieces out. They were, indeed,
covered with blood. The trick was getting deep enough inside
the hole to retrieve the rest and possibly, hopefully, find a
survivor. I wiggled my way in and started working down a
small corridor that was only two feet-wide at its widest. With

Charlie at the opening of the hole talking to me, I kept digging.

The more I dug, the more I found.

More and more blood-covered papers appeared. Papers, but no survivor. After about an hour inside this hole, I came across some torn fabric. Torn fabric, but what kind? Was a survivor near-by? Was this part of their torn clothing? Was I near someone in jeopardy?

I kept digging and then I found it. A human hand – attached to an arm. Although with so much debris around, it was difficult to tell whether or not it was attached. I was in an enclosed area and the smell of death was getting stronger and beginning to have an effect on me. More of a stench than a smell. The stench of peril. Of doom.

I decided to take a breather. I told Charlie I was coming out. I couldn't come out until I told my replacement exactly where I had discovered the hand and arm. I wished it was still attached to a body, but until the body was extricated, there was no way of knowing.

I am somewhat claustrophobic so I welcomed the break. In reality, I was becoming apprehensive of another collapse because we were still in a collapse zone. Every time I heard a squeak, a crack, or a bang, my fear escalated and my heart pounded. It was unnerving.

Getting out of the hole was no easy task. I stand almost six foot one inches tall and weigh in at over two hundred sixty pounds. I had to exit the hole upside down and backwards. Slowly and methodically I worked my way towards the monitor-sized opening at the entrance. Just as I was ready to make my final push out, I came across a blue vinyl duffel bag. I had no idea what was in the bag, so I just handed it to Charlie and exited the hole.

I had removed my helmet because the hole was too small. Then I heard an all too familiar voice yelling out, "What are the Goddamn chances of running into you here?"

I got to my feet, turned around and there was my old friend Brian Durr standing on a ledge directly above me. I made my way over and hugged him. The embrace brought back memories of Brian's and my incredible past . . .

~~

I met Brian in the autumn of 1979. I was in my firehouse, Hose 2, on a Sunday morning. Each Sunday morning someone was designated to bring bagels, and this was my Sunday.

I arrived at 8:30 that morning and went to the kitchen to get a bowl for the bagels. One by one, other members started arriving. Rich Spinoccia, Frank Musso, George Mulholland to name just a few. Other members from outside the company also started pouring in. Abe Brodsky from Rescue Company, Lee Tucholski from Hose 3, and Charlie Ricciardelli from Engine Company were regulars on Sunday mornings. After bagels, we went out to do truck wash and truck maintenance.

It was now 11:30, and I noticed a tan Jeep Wrangler pull up to the East Side of the firehouse. Two people got out and walked up to us. They were from the Bethpage Fire Department and their names were John Castles and Brian Durr. They introduced themselves and told us the Nassau County Fire Commission was holding a benefit hockey game with all proceeds going to the Nassau County Burn Center. We invited them inside and began to talk. Brian and I connected almost immediately.

Brian and I are a bit larger than normal. We're both tall, a little over-weight, and we both love hockey. "We're looking for more players," he said.

I told him I played, and he invited me to the next practice at Cantiague Park in Hicksville, New York.

I attended 11 p.m. practice in Hicksville the following Saturday. I arrived at 10:15 p.m. and went inside. There was Brian, and he wasted no time introducing me to the rest of the team. I met Al Schwartz and Hal Joseph from the

Hicksville Fire Department. They befriended me right away, and jokingly, they told me to be wary of Brian.

Brian and I got our equipment on and made our way to the ice. We were the last two on the ice. When we stepped on, the rest of the team greeted me, including Freeport Firefighters Joe and Peter Licata, who were also asked to play. This was a pleasant surprise because I felt like I had known these firefighters for an eternity, but in reality, I had just recently met them. I went through several skating drills and then we scrimmaged.

My first shift on the ice was memorable. I scored a goal within the first thirty seconds and managed to play well from then on. After practice we went into the locker room to shower and change. Then head coach Wally asked to see me. I met him by the front door of the rink, and he invited me to play for the rest of the season. I was ecstatic. Me, invited to play out the season with a team I felt at home on almost immediately. I went home and told my parents, then called Valerie, my ex-wife, and my brothers.

Team practices continued in preparation for the big game – us, the Nassau County Fire Marshal's office team, vs. the All-Star team from the Nassau County Police Department. The game was set, a battle of two New York hockey teams. Fun sure, but we wanted to win. That was back on April 18, 1980. And that day was so far removed from what lay before us now . . .

~~

After Brian and I embraced, we got back to the task at hand. The brutal truth of the recent events was omnipresent. We continued digging through the seemingly limitless debris field. The stench of decaying flesh was almost overwhelming, but we knew we had to continue.

After a short break, Brian and I started digging again, side by side. It seemed we knew what the other was thinking or was about to do. We continued on the same pile that I had just come out of. When I exited the hole, another FDNY firefighter had gone into the hole to continue trying to uncover the body.

Brian and I decided to dig in an area just above where we thought the other firefighter might be. We were digging with little results. Everything we tried to move seemed gnarled together and the digging never seemed to end. When we did get a piece out, our moods changed more because we felt we had achieved something, or at least we were moving forward. After about an hour, we uncovered a hole the size of a basketball. We could clearly see down inside the hole to where the firefighter had uncovered more of a body.

We saw a twisted mangled body that was lifeless, covered with blood and unrecognizable. Even after years of fire fighting, it was a shocking sight. We made the hole bigger so another firefighter could fit down inside the hole. He began handing out everything in sight when all of a sudden he stopped, turned his head, and vomited.

"Are you okay?" I asked.

"Yes." He pointed to a woman's leg attached to her torso with a steel-reinforcing bar piercing her body. It was dreadful and turned my stomach. To get the woman out of the hole we had to call in one of the welders. He had to cut the main portion of the steel frame away from her body so we could remove her. I kept a small piece of that beam that was small enough to fit into the pocket of my turnout pants.

After the beam was removed, we placed the body in a body bag and took it down off the pile. We continued working to retrieve her other leg, but it was nowhere to be found. Brian and I kept working in the same area when all of a sudden, he yelled, "Jon."

I looked at him, and he threw me a hockey puck he had found. Brian always had a way to make light of any situation, and this was no different. We started talking about our strategy for the hockey game – now so long ago . . .

~~

We knew the Police department had some terrific players and one prolific scorer named Steve Shoshay. We even went to one of their practices to watch and see how good he really was.

We walked into the Newbridge Road Park Ice Rink and watched from the upper level. We were not surprised as we quickly realized we were going to have our hands full. Brian was the team captain so it was up to him, along with the coach, how we would play this team. The general consensus was if we played offense scoring goals, rather than defense, we stood a better chance of winning. Winning was a microcosm as long as we made a good showing and made the fire service look good doing it.

Game day had arrived. April 18, 1980. Cantiague Park in Hicksville, New York, was the venue chosen to defend our honor and that of our brother firefighters. The rink itself was symmetrical oval shaped. There was seating for about three thousand. The game was slated to start at 1 p.m.

We arrived at 10:30 a.m. One by one, our teammates arrived at the rink and entered the locker room to get dressed. We went out for warm-ups and then returned to the locker room. Vinnie Greco from Greco Brothers Fuel Oil had donated new jerseys. We were dressed to kill.

At 12:30 we went back onto the ice for official introductions. After it was acknowledged that the donation to the Nassau County Burn Center was in excess of ten thousand dollars, the crowd roared with approval. I was chosen to take the ceremonial first face off with Steve Shoshay from the Nassau County Police department. New York Islander John Tonelli dropped the puck with Steve Shoshay winning the face off.

This should have been an omen of what was coming. The game was nearly uneventful until only five minutes remained in the second period. Sluggish, we were losing 2-0.

So much for playing the game offensively. Our goalie, Joe Licata from Freeport, had been making some extraordinary saves. He had just made another great save when Vinnie from the police department took a cheap shot at Joe while he was down on the ice. No penalty was called. Play was stopped, and we had a face-off to Joe's right. Brian and I looked at each other and silently nodded in agreement we had to do something to spark our team. The referee dropped the puck, and I leveled Vinnie the police officer. He came up swinging. We fought and were broken up within fifteen seconds. We made our way to the penalty boxes for the start to a staring contest. This was the spark we needed. The period ended and when we came out for the third period, we all had renewed attitudes.

We played hard, hit hard and defended hard. With about eight minutes left in the game, we were still down 2-0. Brian made a great defensive play and passed the puck to me as I broke for the blue line. He put the puck right on my stick from about fifty feet away, and I had a breakaway (one on one against the goalie). I skated like I was being chased by a crazed dog and scored on a blistering wrist shot from about twenty feet out. Brian and I both stepped up our games. He kept making great defensive plays, passing me the puck, and I kept scoring. I scored all four of my goals within six minutes in the final period. My last goal came on a slap shot from about ten feet out which tied the game. The Nassau County Police department scored another goal with only thirty seconds remaining to win the game. We were devastated. They were elated. After ten minutes of standing ovation in which people stood five deep at the boards, an announcement was made that over five thousand people had witnessed the competition.

We shook hands at center ice and congratulated each other for a well-played game. I found new respect for their team. They'd played with resolve and deserved to win. My team started leaving the ice, and I followed. When I got to the gate, I stepped through and the referee grabbed my arm and asked me to stay for a minute. Chief Finkelman, who worked for the Nassau County Fire Marshal's office and is also an instructor at the fire service academy, asked the crowd for their attention. With that, he announced that I had been named the Most Valuable Player for the game, even though we lost. I received a ten-minute standing ovation. I cried like a baby. This was an unexpected honor that I have cherished ever since. I will remember that day always – because it was my finest game ever . . .

~~

When Brian threw me the puck at Ground Zero, I reminisced for a couple of minutes about the game, and then continued on with our work on the pile. But mentally, I had to go other places to keep working. I flashed back again to September 1981 . . .

~~

Valerie and I had been married for about a year and a half. Brian and Cecilia had just been married. Cecilia was a New York City police officer and was working in Brooklyn. I was home in my apartment on Pearsall Avenue in Freeport when my telephone rang. Brian wanted us to go out with him and Cecilia to celebrate her new appointment as an instructor at the New York City Police Academy.

We agreed to meet at Ruffy's Steak House in Syosset, New York at eight that evening. As we sat down for dinner, Cecilia's pager interrupted our small talk several times, and she kept getting up to make telephone calls. I found this somewhat peculiar, but who was I to question it.

We finished our meal and decided to call it a night. On the way home, Valerie said she also thought the phone calls and Cecilia leaving the table during dinner were odd, almost to the point of being suspicious, like Cecilia had something to hide.

Things remained uneventful until Brian's birthday in April, 1983. I remember him telling me the previous January that he was going to have a birthday party like no other. When April arrived, Brian called and reminded me of the upcoming party. I had not seen him in several weeks and was excited, even though I knew something was amiss. I didn't know then that this was the beginning of the end of both our marriages.

When I got to his house for the party, Brian was already inebriated. His brothers Wayne and Peter they told me Brian had caught his wife being unfaithful. This had to be devastating to Brian and I was determined to help him any way I could. Brian had been such a great friend over the years. I decided it was my turn to be a good friend.

As the night continued, Brian got drunk to the point we had to chase him down the street and calm him down. He broke down and let it all out about how he had suspected her for years of being unfaithful. He told us whenever he confronted her, she denied it, until he caught her red handed. Their marriage was over. Brian's heart was broken. So was mine.

I was also experiencing marital problems. Over the course of the next two and a half years, Brian and I spent more time together. Because of what had happened to him, I think subconsciously I started having doubts about my own marriage. I was married to an only child, and I was a middle child who suffered from the "middle child syndrome." Brian and I would go out on drinking binges, and even though I was already a father, I felt I needed to be there for Brian, while trying to meet my own emotional needs.

In September 1984, Brian and I were participating in the Labor Day Parade and Drill in Hicksville, New York. We would compete against each other for our respective departments. After we marched in the parade we met at the beer tent. This was a predetermined meeting where we knew we would drink copious amounts of beer and get completely drunk.

When we met, I'd already had several beers and was well on my way to self-destruction. Brian was the driver of his apparatus, therefore he knew he had to be cautious about drinking. After the parade ended, all of the fire trucks had been parked in the rear of the Mid Island Mall in Hicksville, which was on the East Side. The block party after the parade was on the West Side of the mall. We proceeded to party hearty.

I have always been somewhat of a practical joker, so after about two hours of fun, I decided to play a practical joke on Brian. I knew where his fire truck was parked. I excused myself to go the bathroom and made my way over to the East Side of the mall. Almost two hundred additional fire trucks from all over the East Coast had arrived to take part in the annual Labor Day celebration. Finding his truck would be no easy task. I began searching up and down the endless rows of fire trucks when I really had to go to the bathroom. Because there were none in sight, I found a secluded spot and relieved myself. When I looked up, much to my surprise, right in front of me was Bethpage Fire Department Engine Company 944 staring me in the face.

Fire trucks don't have keys to start their engines, and I couldn't resist the chance to drive people crazy and have them try to explain what happened to their fire truck. I found the battery switch, turned on the ignition switch, and pushed the start button. The roar of the diesel was deafening, but music to my ears. I became nervous when one of the security people came over and asked if everything was okay. I was in uniform, and he obviously didn't know the difference between a Bethpage Fire Department uniform and a Freeport Fire Department uniform. They look incredibly alike. The fun was just beginning.

I pulled the truck out of the spot and moved it about

one half mile away. I longed to see the look on Brian's face when he returned to find his fire truck missing. How was he going to explain this to his chief?

It didn't matter. I said goodbye to Brian at 11 p.m. and headed for home. While walking to our truck, I heard a rumor that a fire truck had been stolen from the parking lot. Hmmm, and a grin.

About two months later, I was in Bethpage at Brian's firehouse on a Saturday afternoon. Brian and I were bored. The chiefs were out of town at a symposium on public safety, and Brian felt it would be okay to take Engine 944 and Ladder 904 out for driver's practice. At the time it didn't matter that I wasn't a member of the Bethpage Fire Department. We started up the trucks and proceeded down Stewart Avenue towards the local delicatessen for lunch. Much to our surprise, Deputy Chief Frank DeBobes was inside. He didn't attend the symposium and elected to stay in town that weekend. When we walked in and saw him, we looked at each other without saying a word. We knew we would be in serious trouble if we were caught. We were petrified. We did our best to misdirect his attention, and got our lunch.

Brian had more to lose than I did. If we had been caught, he would have certainly been expelled from the Bethpage Fire Department, and I would have been arrested for stealing a fire truck, effectively ending both our fire department careers. We walked out of the deli, up to the trucks, and drove away quickly before Chief DeBobes came outside. We returned to the firehouse and put the trucks away. We managed to dodge the bullet then, but looking back I realized I was not proud of my actions during the incidents. My own problems should have had no bearing on the manner in which I represented my firehouse . . .

~~

Brian and I continued digging through the pile, finding everything from small pieces of concrete to chunks of steel the size of buses. After a half-hour, Charlie Manning, another member of my crew, came over to us with bottles of water. The air was so dusty that we had to continually hydrate ourselves, wash our faces off, and repeatedly wipe our eyes. When water was poured over our heads, it looked like a mudflow coming off our foreheads and arms. When he handed the bottle of water to me, he asked what he should do with the duffel bag we had found a couple of hours before. He handed me the bag, and I asked Brian to take a look inside with me.

I opened the bag and found a couple of notebooks with handwritten notes on them. I opened one up and started reading it. It contained notes about terrorism. I told Brian to look at it and when he did, his reaction was the same. Complete disbelief. Could we have found some important piece of evidence? Who did this duffel bag belong to? Were there clues to the attack in the writings? Who wrote them? Were they still alive? Were they among us?

Without wasting another second, I took the duffel bag to my chief, John Wensley. I told him to take a look. He did and had the same reaction that Brian and I had. He asked where we found it, and I told him. He said he would turn it over to the proper authorities. Chief Wensley is a Freeport Police Officer, so I was confident he would handle it properly. I believe it was turned over to the FBI for analysis.

I returned to the pile where Brian and I met up with some of my brother firefighters from Freeport. They had formed their own assembly line for removing debris. I grabbed a stack of spackle buckets, one of thousands used for removing small debris, and put them down next to a piece of steel box beam measuring about 3 by 5 feet at its base. It was standing up on a diagonal and protruded about one hundred feet in the air. Next to the beam was what looked like another void. I decided to climb down into this void and start searching again.

Each time we arrived at Ground Zero, we were met by one of the chief's aids who was charged with directing all incoming personnel. Just prior to our driving under the catwalk that connected the Millennium Hotel to one of the other buildings of the Trade Center, the aid approached us and told all of us to roll up our sleeves. We all complied and this chief's aide, with indelible marker, wrote our individual social security numbers on each of our forearms. He told us that this was still a collapse zone and they had to be able to identify us in case of another collapse and we were killed or trapped. He also told us if we had cell phones, we should carry them with us. In case of a collapse, if we were buried under rubble, the ringing of our cell phones might help locate us. That was a sobering thought that still makes me shake.

I started working my way down inside this 3 x 5-foot solid steel box beam. When I shone my hand light inside the beam, I saw smaller pieces of mangled bar joists and steel reinforcement rods. I slowly worked my way down about thirty feet inside the pile. I estimated I was now about ten feet below street level. I kept working my way in, the entire time talking to my Lieutenant, Frank Tucker. He was at the top of the box beam, and we continued communication the entire time.

Suddenly I felt the ground shaking. Everything around me felt like it was moving. I was completely frozen in fear. I told Frank immediately and remained absolutely still and silent, unable to move in any direction. I began thinking that this may be the end for me. I thought about my children, my wife, my parents, my in laws, and my brother firefighters. I started praying like never before until I heard what sounded like a whistle. Up above me, Frank had told everyone that something might be moving. What happened next is truly amazing considering the size of the situation and the thousands of firefighter and rescue workers in the immediate area. Everyone made the "shhhhhhhh" sound. The entire Ground Zero area fell silent. I could actually hear my own breathing and the breathing of the people thirty feet above me. I was scared beyond anything I could have possibly imagined. I was mentally preparing for the end. I begged God for forgiveness for all my sins. Suddenly I felt an assured calm about me. In my heart, my soul, and my thoughts, I felt I was about to die.

After a minute of silence, Frank told me the rumbling was probably caused by one of the huge cranes that was in the process of being placed. I let out a sigh of relief, my eyes welled up with tears, and I trembled. I managed to keep it to myself. I knew I had to keep searching for survivors, so I kept looking for the next thirty minutes or so, but my efforts were mired in disappointment. I began to climb out of the hole and when I got to the top and escaped, my brother firefighters were there to greet me. I hugged the first one I saw. I was grateful to be alive, and I will never take my job for granted again.

I began taking my failure to find any survivors personally. I knew six of the people who were missing, and I made it my mission in life to find at least one of them. My frustration was mounting and my patience diminishing. I thought of my own shortcomings and how I would explain to my family how I failed to find anyone. That possibility was intolerable.

I took a breather and went back to the heavy rescue truck for a drink. When I got there I sat down and surveyed everything. I noticed by now the people in charge had placed several land surveyors with transits (leveling equipment) at various locales around the site. Having been born and raised in the construction business, I quickly realized why. They had their sights set on very precise areas around Ground Zero and were watching to make sure nothing else would move. If one of the other unstable buildings were to collapse, the loss of life would be demoralizing. We would lose thousands more than we already had. Unacceptable.

Brian came over and asked if I was okay. I gave him a look that only a firefighter could understand. He knew how scared I was, and his gaze made me feel better. He understood.

Brian told me he had been relieved from duty for the day and that he was going home with Chief Campbell. I told him I would be in touch, we embraced, and I watched him walk away knowing how lucky he and I were to be alive. We had come through another day.

# Jon's father

The first medic course graduates in NY State for volunteer firefighters

L – R; Artie Rasmussen, **Emory Wright**, Augie Schmidt, County Executive Ralph Caso,Les Fieldsa, Benny Pandolfo, Bill Casmasina.

## Three

# Rookie School

WE have just arrived at the final staging area before actually entering Ground Zero. I pulled the heavy rescue truck up next to an FDNY Engine company. I looked at the Engine Company and the numbers 219 were on the side. How ironic was this? I was driving Freeport Heavy Rescue truck 219! I parked beside them. Captain Bentley, Lieutenant Tucker, Charlie Manning, Charlie McEneany, Chief Wensley, each looked at one another and were flabbergasted. FDNY Engine Company 219 was operating right next to us – pumping water to the tower ladder that was operating on the burning pile inside the perimeter. We had parked next to the one truck in the entire New York City Fire Department that had the same number delineation as our truck. What a rush!

Chief Wensley ordered us to stand by. He spoke to Deputy Chief Joseph DiBernardo at the command post and waited for orders. I watched him vigilantly and made a mental note of the look on his face when he turned and looked back at us.

Meanwhile, we waited at the truck for orders and tried to pass the time. One by one, huge tractor-trailers along with two rather large cranes passed us to position themselves to enter Ground Zero.

We were at a dead-end street about one hundred fifty feet from the Hudson River and were milling around for the first hour. I approached the pump operator of FDNY Engine

219 and struck up a conversation with him. He and his brother firefighters were as amazed as we were that our trucks had the same number.

When I looked behind the heavy rescue truck, I observed a war zone. I still have difficulty believing I'd been able to maneuver the truck through the debris and thick dust that permeated the entire area. The dust was six inches thick in some places. It looked like a scene from the Tom Hanks movie *Saving Private Ryan*, as though a bomb had been dropped, which is essentially what happened. Eerie clouds had settled onto the ground, around the fallen debris, everywhere. At least Hanks and his men knew they were in a war zone. This had been a bustling metropolitan area just hours before. Now, just devastation. Ruin.

I remember my foot touching the accelerator of the truck, looking in the rear view mirror, and seeing a veritable dust storm. The truck exhaust made everything behind us impassible. Visibility was zero and no one could go anywhere until the dust settled. Ultimately, I developed a chronic cough.

On one occasion, I repositioned the truck to let one of the cranes pass us into Ground Zero. When I finished backing up to my original parking spot, a group of firefighters from FDNY Rescue 1 walked past us. In that group were two of the Freeport Fire Department premier firefighters, Frank Fee and Paul Hashagen. While Frank Fee acknowledged us with a nod of his head as he passed, Paul Hashagen stopped, shook hands and said hello to each of us.

Frank acknowledged us once again and the two of them kept walking. I have personally known Frank Fee my entire life. I have known Paul Hashagen for over twenty-five years. Paul is a former chief of the Freeport Fire Department and when he was chief, we butted heads on more than one occasion.

On this day, none of that mattered. In the aftermath of my tour at Ground Zero, I have come to realize what a difficult task it was for those two intrepid and altruistic firefighters to manage a smile in such horrible conditions. Both had been at Ground Zero almost from the onset and had to be physically and emotionally debilitated.

When they passed out of sight, Lieutenant Tucker, Captain Bentley and I appreciated the fact that they had acknowledged us under such lamentable conditions. I wondered if I would ever see them alive again, given the circumstances. I understood that if anyone were to be found alive, these two valiant firefighters could find them. I wish I could have worked side by side with them, because I would have learned many things.

What we were about to do began to set in emotionally. Pain and repudiation was etched on the faces of every rescue worker we encountered. I thought to myself, Will I be able to handle all of this? Will I crack under pressure? How will I react when I find a body or worse, body parts?

I was the senior member of this crew, and I had a responsibility to maintain my composure and poise at all times. Other men in my crew would be looking to me and follow my lead, so I had to be in control of my emotions. I went inside the back of the heavy rescue truck and just sat for a few minutes. I didn't want my brothers to see I was uncomfortable because that would have been disastrous to them as well as me, not to mention counterproductive. When I emerged, I had my act together and got back to the job at hand.

I began talking to Captain Bentley and made some suggestions about how I thought he should separate the crew once inside Ground Zero. He suggested we take a wait-and-see attitude, because we didn't know what we would encounter once inside. Dave always seems calm and collected and is a very easy going individual. Dave was just being Dave, and that was fine with me. I was honored to work side by side with him at Ground Zero.

I started walking around the entryway to survey the area. When I turned, I saw Kevin and Timmy Muldowney standing at the barricade trying to enter Ground Zero. They had been rebuffed because they were not FDNY firefighters, although Kevin is a NYPD detective. Their brother Richie Muldowney was one of the valiant firefighters missing at Ground Zero. Richie had also worked for me in my construction business before he got the job with the FDNY. Their brother-in-law Tommy Andello was standing there with them.

When they saw me standing and looking at them, their pain became unmistakable. I felt it, and I am certain they felt mine. I got a knot in my stomach as they walked over to me because I didn't know what to say to any of them. Without saying a word, I embraced each one of them.

Then Timmy Muldowney asked the burning question, "Can we come inside Ground Zero on the fire truck with you?"

I was stunned. I didn't know how to answer him. When we left Freeport for Ground Zero, Chief Wensley made it clear that we would be the only ones from Freeport to go to Manhattan. No exceptions.

Chief Wensley was inside Ground Zero at the command post, and I had to devise a way to ask him without anyone else knowing what was going on. Chief Wensley's radio delineation was 2101 while I was 219W. I called him on the radio and it went like this. I said, "2101, this is 219W?"

He answered, "Go ahead 219W?"

"2101, we have additional personnel from down south requesting our assistance getting in."

"219W, is that T.M., K.M., or T.A?"

I answered, "Affirmative."

He said yes without hesitation. A sense of relief came from Timmy, Kevin, and Tommy. I told them to stand by and when we were about to enter, get into the back of the truck and put on any gear they could find. As long as I had any say in the matter, they were going to be able to search for their blood brother. I felt a small measure of satisfaction . . .

~~

Thoughts of the bond that firefighters share sent me drifting back to 1972 when I joined the Freeport Fire Department. I was sworn into the department on the first Tuesday of April with my father looking on as I took the oath. My brother, Randy, already a member of Vigilant Hose Company # 2, made it clear he wanted me in Hose 2, and anything else was unsuitable.

When I took the oath, I looked to my left and saw my fathers glistening eyes and an ear to ear grin. He stood proud that his number two son was now part of a firefighting tradition. A long-standing Wright tradition.

I am sad, even a touch poignant, that my grandfather Pop Wright was not there to see it. It would have been great to have three generations there. He and my great uncle Tiny were charter members of Hose 1 and I sat with them on many occasions and listened to their war stories. He passed away in 1968 after sixty years in the Freeport Fire Department. Eveready Hose Company # 1.

My father had been a forty-seven year member of the Freeport Fire Department. I remember my father telling stories about the old days in Truck Company, as it is better known. As a small child, I would run with my father to the firehouse when a call came in. Our house was on Smith Street and the firehouse was on Church Street, three blocks away.

After I took the oath, my father told me I would have fire school every Sunday morning for the next six weeks. This was the beginning of my thirty-year fire department career. Dad's best friend, Bruce Willets was the chief instructor.

Between my dad and Bruce, I knew I had good teachers. They were both former captains of Excelsior Hook and Ladder Company # 1, and knew all the trade secrets of firefighting.

After the swearing-in ceremony and receiving my badges, my ego now out of control, I went downstairs to my company quarters to be congratulated by the members who were there. After I shook the last persons hand, my brother Randy took a full garbage can, placed it conspicuously on the bar, and said, "Rookie, take out the garbage."

Everyone laughed as I carried out his order, and I knew this was a sign of things to come. When I returned from garbage detail, I was ordered into the kitchen to help with the clean up detail, after which I was unceremoniously besprinkled with a water-filled fire extinguisher. I was officially a rookie. Nevertheless, I was yet to have my cherry run, as it is known in the fire service. A cherry run is the first call you ride the truck on.

My cherry run officially occurred after I'd gone home for the night. Just after midnight, a general alarm was transmitted for a box call at Sunrise Highway and Main Street.

I was talking to my mom, who was still awake and waiting for me at home after the swearing in ceremony. The alarm came over the fire radio, I looked at her, and she just said, "Be careful."

I ran out the door, jumped into my car and off I went to get the fire truck. My company fire truck was a Red and White 1957 Mack, the only one of its kind on Long Island. I was the second to arrive at the firehouse. Bill Froggy Sarro was already there. He lived just two blocks away. I got my gear on and waited for our third man. Fire department protocol requires a three-man crew to roll the truck. Kevin Vollmer, my neighbor who is also the company captain, showed up, jumped in the front officer's seat, and off we went with Froggy driving.

Froggy pulled the truck slowly onto the ramp of the firehouse, and made a right turn onto Broadway. Kevin hit the siren and the buckeye, a very loud air horn that worked off the exhaust manifold and Froggy turned on the lights. We screamed down the street towards the call. I stood proud in the jump seat of the truck directly opposite the front seats as it approached the intersection of Sunrise Highway and Main Street only to realize this was a false alarm.

No matter. I was a fireman; there was officially nothing I couldn't do. No obstacle I couldn't overcome. No life I couldn't save. Moreover, I had the badge to prove it! I had, in an established tradition, broken my cherry. We returned to the firehouse, stowed our gear and I went back home, on top of the firefighter world. I was God's gift to the civilized world. What a high!

On Sunday morning I was expected at the firehouse no later than 8 a.m. I would talk about this day for the rest of the week. I was still in high school and when my schoolmates learned of my induction into the fire department, I was besieged with new friends and many, many girls. This was only the beginning.

I arrived at the firehouse at about 7:30 a.m. and was the first one there. I paced in nervous anticipation of my first day of fire school. Captain Vollmer arrived a few minutes later. He grabbed my hand, and asked me to come outside and started going over the equipment on the truck.

I asked him which piece of equipment was the most important, and he told me the hydrant wrench. I looked at him dumbfounded. "Why a hydrant wrench?" He told me in no uncertain terms the hydrant wrench would be the only thing I would need for quite some time.

I asked why, and he told me that I had to start at the bottom and learn the basics before I could even think about going into a fire and grabbing a nozzle. He told me before I had a nozzle, I had to learn how to attach it to a hydrant by myself. Fire department protocol at that time was two men on a hydrant, but because Hose 2 had a reputation for being second to none, I had to learn to do it by myself. He kept drilling this into my head. Day after day. Night after night. Every night I would go to the firehouse and practice grabbing the hydrant wrench, double and single gates, and the Siamese, a device that allows two feeder lines into one. I would visualize myself hitting the hydrant.

He taught me when you hit the hydrant, to always connect both the double and single gates to the hydrant, not just one or the other. In case of a problem with the double gate, you'd still have the single gate on the other side to work with.

He went on to explain that problems occur more expected, mostly because of the age of the hydrants. Fire hydrants malfunction and break regularly. At the scene of a fire, the guy hitting the hydrant is just as important as the nozzle man putting water on the fire.

Most fire trucks carry between 500 and 1000 gallons of water, which under normal circumstances should be enough to put out the average house fire. The only problem with that theory is most house fires expand well above what's considered average, and rarely occur under normal circumstances. Hence the need for more water. If the engine company runs out of water in their tank, they have to resort to another water source. A fire hydrant.

If the fire hydrant doesn't work properly, or the hydrant man makes a mistake, the results can be insidious. Think about it. The hydrant malfunctions, water-flow to the truck stops, the truck tank is already empty, and the pump operator neglected to fill the tank. The nozzle man then loses water in the middle of advancing on the fire and his hose line goes dead. The fire explodes and firefighters are killed. All of this because a hydrant malfunctioned. Either that or the hydrant man made an egregious mistake.

I made it my personal responsibility to know all the equipment on the truck. I couldn't live with myself with a preventable mistake on my conscious. Having that happen would require a calculated response from the chief of the department and my name would be mud, not to mention the guilt involved.

Six people went to fire school that Sunday. We boarded the truck and off we went to Freeport Fireman Field. Fireman Field was a park located on Buffalo Avenue between Sunrise Highway and Merrick Road. It consisted of a tournament arch, tournament track, Little League baseball field, and a big open field that was used for an assortment of different things from parking to block parties.

When we arrived, Excelsior Hook and Ladder Company # 1 was already there setting up for a ladder evolution. Other fire trucks began arriving with their rookies aboard. Hose 4 had Bob Notheis and Kevin Noll. Hose 3 had Bob Cardinale. Hose 1 had Julie Ellison. Hose 3 had Jimmy Butler, and Engine Company had Tommy Smith. We were officially the rookie school for the year 1972. We all knew each other, were high school friends, and some of us were neighbors who shared close friendships.

Today, fire school would consist of ladder operations. Bruce Newbery and Don Mauersberger were running the class from Truck Company. First they had us place ladders up on the tournament arch and climb them. In the construction business, having done a considerable amount of roofing, I had extensive experience climbing ladders. When my turn came, I ascended the ladder effortlessly. Some of the others had problems, but I was already a very accomplished climber. This fact did not get past the instructors from Truck Company. They were apparently annoyed at my ability, so they made me do it again. This time, once I reached the top, they asked me to lock in.

Locking in means placing one leg through the rungs and clamping down on either the rung or the beam (side) of the ladder. I did precisely as they ordered. I locked in, and they decided to use me as an illustration of *why* we lock in. They began shaking the ladder from the bottom in an attempt to shake me loose. I was near the top, and the ladder was angled in such a way that it was impossible for them to move it, let alone dislodge me. The ladder articulated with the tournament arch at about a sixty-degree angle. With my weight leaning on the top, it was virtually impossible for them to make their point. The ladder wouldn't move. This infuriated them. I came down off the ladder and said nothing. I just wanted this to be over, but they were intent on humiliating me.

Next up was climbing the ladder while carrying either a hose line or a tool with us. Again, this was particularly engaging to me because I was already doing this daily at my job. The instructors showed us precisely what they wanted and we each took our turns. Again they made me go last. I found that peculiar if only because some of the others could learn from my experience, but I kept quiet. They gave me a Halligan tool to carry up.

I began my ascent and when I got about one-third up the ladder, Truck Company had two people on the top of the arch. This time the two men at the top of the arch had obviously been ordered to shake the ladder from the top. They started shaking and I kept climbing. The instructors started yelling at me to hurry up, but every step was perilous.

I came close to falling off about two-thirds of the way up. I stopped to compose myself for about five seconds, and the instructors continued to yell out their profanity-laced tirade. I kept climbing. Two rungs from the top I almost fell again. I told the two guys to stop shaking the ladder. That was the wrong thing for me to say. Their intensity increased, and they made reference to my father who had inauspiciously transferred out of Truck Company. That was their biggest mistake.

I got to the top. They both had their hands firmly entrenched on the ladder and were still shaking. They refused to stop, so I slammed the Halligan tool into the top of the ladder exactly where their hands were holding on. I would imagine it felt as though their hands and fingers had been hit with a hammer. They cursed even more and I climbed down the ladder.

When I got to the bottom, again I was silent. I thought back to the long talk I'd had with my father before going to fire school. He told me there might be some members of Truck Company who wanted to make fire school difficult for me. He told me not to take any nonsense, and of course, I always listen to my dad – well, in this case anyway. To this day, I wonder if they harassed me because Emory Wright was my father, and they were effecting some sort of revenge because my father had the gumption to stand up to them.

I turned my thoughts back to the instructor, and realized I'd have to reserve my anger – if only to pass fire school – because if I failed, I would be out of the Freeport Fire Department. This was not an option. I would not tarnish my family name and history in the department.

Next up on the agenda was climbing the one hundred-foot aerial ladder. Climbing up one hundred feet is nothing like climbing a twenty-foot stationary ladder. Truck Company extended the ladder at about a sixty-five degree angle and the instructors had everyone climb it. Once at the top, we were to clip on with a safety belt, lean back, and let go with our hands. You guessed it; they made me go last, which I expected. The others climbed up and all did what was required without incident. Then it was my turn.

While I waited, the other members of Truck Company

continually harassed me, and I have to admit, I was a bit apprehensive, but I was determined to conquer. I started my climb up the one hundred-foot aerial and the chants began immediately. Again they made reference to my dad and again I gave them a look. Unlike the others, I was made to wear an air pack and carry a Halligan tool up the ladder. I concentrated on the task at hand and kept climbing. When I reached the top, I could hear them yelling at the top of their lungs. They told me to clip on, let go with my hands, and lean back, which I did. The very second I leaned back, they changed the angle of the ladder. When I felt it move, I grabbed and held on for dear life! I was petrified. I yelled down to them, "You assholes."

They laughed because they thought it was boisterously entertaining. I however, did not think it was amusing. Through the speaker at the top of the aerial ladder, they told me if I was a real man, I would climb over the top and down the backside of the aerial ladder.

I didn't know if they were kidding or not, but I was clipped in, and if I did slip, I wasn't going to fall. So, over the top I went. Immediately they started screaming as loud as they could for me to stop, but I kept going. My pride was at stake, more than that, really, I knew if I did stop, I would be the subject of unrelenting ridicule. My immediate problem was I still had a Halligan tool in my hand. "What do I do with the tool?" I yelled. They said to drop it. So I did. It went right through the steel wheel-well and punctured the tire. They were clearly unhappy.

I finished my climb down the opposite side and when I got there, the instructors, who had congregated at the turntable of the aerial ladder, just stared at me with contempt. Everyone else was laughing at the instructors for their poor judgment. Fire school came to a close for the day, I boarded Hose 2, and we left. Truck Company's aerial ladder went out of service for about two weeks. Funny, how things happen.

My last name is Wright and my father made his name by being fearless. He was in the roofing business and climbing was his life, and mine too. I learned everything I know about climbing from my father, and on more than one occasion what he taught me saved my life. My father is not a tall man by any standards. He is almost one foot shorter than I am, but in terms of courage and guts, he is a mountain. I owe him more than I could ever tell. He's a lion in a world of the timid . . .

~~

I prayed for some of his strength as we started the slow, methodical and cautious drive into the actual Ground Zero. Chief Wensley called me on the radio and asked me if the truck would fit under the catwalk. I assured him that even if we had to let air out of the tires, we would fit.

With everyone aboard, and Chief Wensley walking in front of us, I started moving the truck ever so slowly. There was debris strewn everywhere, and I didn't want to damage the tires. Not that it mattered. I just wanted to be cautious. I made a right turn and passed FDNY Engine 219 still connected to the steamer connection on the hydrant. About fifty feet past Engine 219 was the catwalk to the Millennium Hotel we had to pass under. As we approached, Chief Wensley was walking backwards in front of us. I opened the driver's side door, stood, leaned out and watched as we inched under the catwalk. We had about three inches to spare. We collectively held our breaths as we passed. I closed the door and we were officially inside Ground Zero. It was 7 p.m.

Once inside, our demeanor changed. We all had cat's eyes, and I was attentive to every detail. Nothing escaped my eye.

As we inched forward, we came to a left turn. On the right was the giant crane that had forced us to move the heavy rescue truck outside Ground Zero so it could pass. The crane was minuscule compared to the Ground Zero area itself. Just in front of the crane was a NYPD cruiser that had been crushed by falling debris. It had "Street Crime" written on its side, and anyone inside the car had probably been crushed to death. No one could have been inside that vehicle and survived. We could see the telltale marks made by a Hurst tool (Jaws of Life), that had been used. Standing between the car and the crane was a group of what looked like construction workers. They all waved in unison as we inched along and yelled, "Good luck."

As I prepared to make the left turn, I spied a rather large wrecking ball directly in front of the truck and had to stop. Chief Wensley had already seen it and was trying to get someone to move it. I watched while he spoke to one of the construction workers, and I said to Captain Bentley that this might take a while. He acknowledged and agreed. Just then, another construction worker walked up to me just as I set the air brake and he asked if we needed the wrecking ball moved. I said yes, and I yelled to the back for everyone to get out and help this guy move the ball.

Everyone piled out and as they got to the front of the truck, they watched as this construction worker named Ben walked up to the wrecking ball the size of a Volkswagen Beetle, put his hands on it, and started rolling it out of the way, completely unassisted. We were astonished at this man's feat of strength. It is truly one of the most amazing things I have ever seen. He was like a kid rolling a beach ball. I couldn't begin to guess how much this wrecking ball weighed, but Ben moved it with relative ease.

I made the left turn past the wrecking ball and at a snails pace, we continued on. Chief Wensley walked in front of us and stopped when he got to the command post. We had traveled only about sixty feet. It seemed as though it took an hour. But in reality, only a few minutes had passed.

Standing at the command post were Battalion Chief

James Corcoran, Deputy Chief John Casey, and Battalion Chief Kevin Burns. Chief Burns talked to Chief Wensley and pointed to where he wanted our truck placed. Chief Wensley gave Chief Burns a look of complete surprise. I couldn't hear what Chief Burns said, but I soon found out. Chief Wensley walked over to me in the driver's seat and told me to reposition the truck. He pointed to the area directly between the remains of Tower One and Tower Two. The main piles were about one hundred fifty feet tall, and the debris field sloped down from there.

A bulldozer arrived to move more debris out of our way and lead us to our final position. Ever so slowly and cautiously I inched the truck forward and as I did so, the chiefs at the command post all gave us an unofficial hand salute. Deputy Chief Casey yelled out, "Good luck and be careful."

It took almost ten minutes for us to reach our final position. When I stopped, the front bumper of Freeport Heavy Rescue truck was directly over the curb of the circular driveway that once connected Tower One and Tower Two of the World Trade Center. We had arrived at Ground Zero — the only fire truck allowed inside the perimeter.

Slowly we made our way off the truck and worked our way to the rear. Chief Wensley told us to stand by and wait for orders. Captain Bentley and I looked at each other and knew how afraid the other was. The same look of fear was on the faces of Lieutenant Tucker, Charlie McEneaney and Charlie Manning. My heart was going one hundred miles an hour, and I felt like I had an apple in my throat as we waited for our orders. I took deep breaths as often as practicable.

Off to the left of the front of the truck, was a piece of skeletal frame of the Trade Center that had either been a projectile from the explosion or been planted vertically in the ground when the towers collapsed. About fifty feet off the ground, hanging from this piece of steel frame was a women's flower print dress. I wondered what happened to the woman that had worn it. Was she alive? If not, where was her body? Did she have a family? Did she have children?

These thoughts infiltrated my mind. I pondered how lucky I was to be married to Dorothy and how terrific my children Brendan and Christian are.

Chief Wensley came over and told us Chief Campbell wanted lights deep inside the pile. I thought that was peculiar at first, until I heard why. Just as we parked the truck, the rescue workers from the FDNY discovered one of their ladder trucks deep inside the pile. Inside the truck were the bodies of six dead firefighters. I thought to myself, "Holy Mother of God, what have I gotten myself into?"

Lt. Tucker took command of this detail. He must have sensed near panic. Because of my climbing experience, he ordered me to accompany him to the top of the pile where the makeshift entrance to the ladder truck was intertwined with the massive steel beams. I followed him up the pile, but because I climbed faster, I passed him. We had to make our way around an unimaginable sight. Before us were huge piles of twisted steel beams and steel reinforcement rods protruding eighty-to-one hundred feet into the air. My mind was mangled by the horror before us.

By now there were probably about three hundred FDNY firefighters, all within a one hundred-yard radius, and all working the bucket lines. When Lt. Tucker and I arrived at the ladder truck, we looked back, and our heavy rescue truck looked as though it was a quarter-mile away. I felt a sense of pride like never before. Ours was the only fire truck visible within Ground Zero. There was not another fire truck in sight. I felt like we had just climbed for an hour, but it had only been ten minutes. I was fatigued. The air was filled with tremendous smoke and dust. At times it was like being inside a burning building. Every breath burned and irritated my throat.

Lt. Tucker decided to use the Circle D lights off our heavy rescue truck. I radioed back to Captain Bentley for the necessary equipment while Lt. Tucker made his way inside the pile to where the ladder truck was.

Firefighters Charlie Manning and Charlie McEneaney started up the pile with the necessary equipment. Neither was adept at climbing but there was an abundance of FDNY firefighters to help them with the equipment. It was incredible to see the FDNY firefighters helping our brothers. No longer did it matter who was a professional firefighter and who was a volunteer.

Lt. Tucker yelled up for me to come inside the pile. I waited until our equipment arrived and then proceeded inside the pile with the circle D light, Charlie McEneaney feeding in the power supply with help from the FDNY firefighters. I plugged it in and lit up the immediate area. I could clearly see the remains of the truck that had been crushed to about three feet tall with the six men inside.

I thought, God give me the strength. I fed the electric line down to the others who were working so hard to free their brethren. I handed off the light and when it lit, clearly visible was the word "FIRE" on what remained of the left of the side of the truck. I turned away, closed my eyes, and said a quick prayer for these lost firefighters. I was numb and frightened.

I felt fortunate because there were so many FDNY firefighters, we decided to start looking elsewhere. In the meantime, we observed an endless supply of people carrying red bags down off the pile. We talked about that for a short time when one of the other FDNY firefighters told us the red bags contained body parts. I thought, Oh great, this is what we have to look forward to . . .

~~

Images of those red bags took me back to 1974. Within a six-week period, five people had committed suicide on the

tracks of the Long Island Railroad that is directly across from
Freeport Fire Department Headquarters.

The first time we were called, we arrived at the base of
the platform, which is elevated above street level, and were
told that someone had jumped in front of a train. Being one
of the youngest on the crew, I was told to stand by the truck
and wait for orders from the officer in charge, who in this
case was Lt. Ed Martin. We responded to the call with only a
driver, the officer in charge, and me.

Lt. Martin went up the stairs to the platform and
confirmed that someone had indeed died on the tracks. He
ordered me up the stairs with a shovel and plastic bags. The
Freeport Police Department was already on the scene, and
the Long Island Railroad Police were responding.

When I got to the top of the stairs, Lt. Martin took me
aside and told me that the scene was gruesome and that the
person who died was torn apart by the collision with the train
and in many pieces. He asked me if I could handle this, and I
told him I thought I could. He told me the third rail, which
sends high voltage to operate the trains had been shut down,
and that it was safe to climb down under the stopped train.
He told me to be prepared for what I was about to see and to
take the shovel with me.

What I saw scared the hell out of me. I saw a person's
body in countless pieces – obviously dead. A leg here, an arm
there, internal organs lodged in the framework of the train
car. Just as I climbed under the train, the Long Island
Railroad Police showed up with red plastic bags. These police
officers had apparently been through this scenario before,
and they told me to use the shovel to pick up the pieces and
place them in the red plastic bags. "One body part in one
bag", he kept saying to me. He must have known I was
rookie because he said it over and over again. I remember
getting a little squeamish when I picked up what I thought to
be a right arm. It was mangled almost beyond recognition.

The skin had been torn off and the bones exposed. I remember managing to keep my composure and finishing the job.

When I emerged from under the train, I was covered in blood. While under the train, I'd clambered around on my stomach because there was not much room. I was barely able to move.

We finished the call and returned to the firehouse. During the course of the call, about five other firefighters showed up and when the call was over, everyone left without uttering a word. It was as though this had been just another call. I went home and couldn't sleep so I went for a walk for two hours. I walked to the duck pond next to the high school and just sat there thinking about it. I knew couldn't let anyone know how much it bothered me, but it kept eating away.

I went home and laid there staring at the ceiling until the sun came up, then I went to work. It bothered me for weeks, but no one seemed willing to talk to me about it, so I kept quiet. It bothered me to no end, but I knew I had to be mentally tough and not let on.

During the next five weeks, four other people committed suicide on those very same tracks and on all four occasions, I was there to pick up the pieces. It was a time I will never forget. I still wonder about those people, why they would do such a drastic thing to end their lives, and about how it has affected me . . .

~~

That concern was partly a motivation to find live bodies. Due in large part to the location of our heavy rescue truck, we were constantly utilized with our specialized equipment for myriad assignments.

We were called to a location to use our air tools to cut away some sheet metal that was on top of what they thought might be a body. When I got to that location, the smell of death was in the air. The putrid smell of decaying flesh.

Lt. Frank Tucker and I started using the pneumatic hacksaw to cut away some of the sheet metal. It was not working very well, but it was all we had at the time. After about fifteen minutes of uninterrupted cutting, I took a short break. I looked over to the command post and could see all the battery-operated reciprocating saws whose batteries had gone dead. There was no way to charge the batteries at Ground Zero because everything had been destroyed – thus the need to utilize our equipment. This was the case throughout the night.

When I went back to cutting with the pneumatic hack saw, I decided that repugnant odor was getting stronger, and I needed to confirm that we were looking in the right spot. I called for a cadaver-sniffing dog, and within two minutes, an NYPD police officer was on the scene with his German shepherd. When I called for the dog, my words echoed from where we stood to where the dogs were standing by. Everyone yelled out, "We need a dog," and that was that. The dog's handler came up, asked what we had. I told him I thought we might have a body here. He told me to stand by and commanded to his dog, Mercury, "Find."

Mercury made his way under the enormous steel box beam that we were forced to work around, crawled about three feet into the hole, came out in about five seconds, and just sat. The handler said, "You have a hit," meaning we had indeed found another body. Sitting in that spot was Mercury's way of saying we found something. It was an awesome sight watching Mercury work. Diligent and unrelenting, the dog was a portrait in courage and determination.

The handler called to Mercury and the dog went right over to him. They went down off the pile to take a break. A couple of other FDNY firefighters followed Mercury and his handler down to the command post. That was the last I ever saw of them.

Four

# Otto and AAA Development

I was at the back of the heavy rescue truck putting my gear back on. I'd just rinsed my eyes for what seemed to be the fiftieth time. The constant deluge of dust and noxious gases coming from the two piles was almost two much to bear. Every time I blew my nose I felt pain that brought new meaning to the word Technicolor. I wondered what this dust was that we were all breathing.

On the inside of the heavy rescue truck, we had cabinets filled with specialized heavy rescue equipment, and a rather large inventory of Basic Life Support and Advanced Life Support medical supplies and equipment. The truck is usually stocked with at least ten bottles of saline to be used for everything from cleaning cuts to rinsing burns and eyes to just pouring over our heads for cooling off purposes. Within four hours, every bottle was gone.

I took a twenty-minute break to lie down in the back of the heavy rescue truck and rest, fatigued beyond words. Once I got up off the floor, I was like new again. I tried to call home, but I didn't harbor much hope I would get through. It was certainly worth a try. I had tried previously, but was unsuccessful.

I knew my wife was working, so I pulled my cell phone out of my pocket and called my sister-in-law, Janet, at her job at Ithaca College. Much to my surprise, she answered and asked me, "Where are you?"

I told her I was at Ground Zero and immediately sensed uneasiness in her voice. She must have told me to "Be careful" ten times. I told her I'd be okay and that it was unlike anything I had ever seen or experienced before.

Just then I got called to go back out to relieve Lt. Tucker. I told Janet I had to go, she told me again that she loved me and for me to be careful. I told her to tell everyone that I loved them also and not to worry because I was going to be fine.

I called Captain Bentley and asked him what he wanted Charlie Manning and me to do. With his ever-present grin, he pointed to the pile and said, "Up there," and off we marched. I looked over my shoulder, he was still grinning as we ascended the pile. He was on one of the bucket lines and seemed content just being Dave. I've known Dave Bentley for more than twenty years, long before he joined the fire department. His demeanor hasn't changed at all over that time, and I am honored to be his friend and brother firefighter.

When Charlie and I were climbing up, I spied a chunk of steel that looked very much like a radiator from an old house. I found it puzzling that such an item would be found here, but after I thought about it, I realized it could have come from anywhere. It could have been inside one of the civilian trucks that were destroyed during the collapse, or maybe it was sitting on the sidewalk. I don't know how it got there, but it brought thoughts of my friend Otto . . .

~~

I first met Otto Pulse from Massepequa, NY in November, 2000. I was introduced to him through an attorney friend of mine, Frank Cositore. Otto had retained Frank's law firm, Cositore & LoPresti to represent him in a civil law suit in regards to Otto's building being burned down and the Massepequa Fire Department allegedly letting it burn.

Otto hired me to prove his case through the analyzing of

forensic evidence, all related to the fire service. I was hired to get information from the Massepequa Fire District, requesting the information through the Freedom of Information Act. I had the know-how to ask the right questions and get the information even though the Massepequa Fire District wanted no part of me. It would be fair to say I made the Massepequa Fire District's life a living hell.

When I met Otto, the meeting was set up through a telephone call. I went to his temporary offices in the back building on his property where the main building had burned. On the telephone, I detected a southern accent and was curious to meet him.

The meeting was set for November 27, 2000. I arrived and found the building on the north side of the Long Island Railroad parking lot about three hundred feet from Broadway. When I stood in front of the building, I looked to the left and off in the distance, about three hundred feet away was the headquarters for the Massepequa Fire Department. That got my attention.

I walked down the driveway to the rear building and knocked on the door. "Come in," a female voice yelled. When I entered, I saw an office with four desks and plenty of chairs.

Out from behind the door at the back walked a tall, imposing man with glasses, a cowboy hat, and gray hair. He looked at me and said, "Hi, I'm Otto Pulse, and those bastards across the street burned my building down."

"What bastards?" I asked without missing a breath

"The Massapequa Fire Department."

"How do you know that?" I asked.

"Because you're going to prove it," Otto replied.

This guy is out of his mind if he thinks I'm going after the Massapequa Fire Department, I thought. He invited me into his office and we began a three-hour discussion. I wanted to know what proof he had and why he thought the Massapequa Fire Department would do this.

He explained to me exactly what he thought. My first impression of Otto was that he was a nutcase. As I continued to talk to him, I began to realize the man was a genius. He was concise and detailed about the events that led up to his building burning down.

I found his description of the events comical at times, but even more so, I found him to be absolutely truthful. I explained to Otto what my fee would be and he agreed right away. I told him the first thing I would do was gather information about the Massapequa Fire Department. I left for home to start working.

On the way home, I wondered what motive the Massapequa Fire Department could possibly have to burn his building down. I decided my first information request would be for the audiotape of the fire that the Massapequa Fire Department made. I sent that request off with another request for additional paperwork and realized it would take a couple of weeks to get back. While I waited, I decided I would interview some of Otto's tenants in the hope they could shed some light on the fire.

What they told me scared the hell out of me.

I first interviewed a man named Charlie. The first time I spoke to Charlie on the phone, he told me that during the fire, he witnessed Massapequa firefighters throwing cast iron radiators out of the second floor window.

I asked him if the radiators were burning and he told me no, which didn't surprise me at all. Cast iron is not combustible. Then I asked him to describe what he saw. He said "They were throwing everything in sight out of the second floor window."

Again, this didn't surprise me.

He went on to explain how the firefighters appeared to be aiming things at the pile of debris already on the ground.

I found that odd and asked him, "Why do you think they were doing that?"

His answer mortified me. "They were aiming at the pile because they were trying to hit our musical instruments," he said boisterously. Again I asked, "Why?"

His response made me nauseous. He said he heard the firefighter's voices, and they were saying things like, "Hit those fucking instruments, we don't want those hippies living here again." And, "Their kind make the whole neighborhood unattractive."

Right then I excused myself and walked outside. Was I hearing things? Was this guy telling the truth or was he making this all up, and why would he make it up? None of this made any sense to me. I thought to myself, I've been a firefighter for twenty-eight years and I have never seen or heard anything like this ...

~~

On October 14, 2001, my next-door neighbor's house burned up.

This had been a particularly difficult day for me as I had just returned from another Ground Zero tour. We were unsuccessful searching for survivors, and I was starting to realize there would be none.

I was fatigued when I arrived home and took a shower, had something to eat, and planned to go to bed. I sat on my recliner and tried to unwind, but the day's events made relaxing impossible. It was a balmy night, so I went for a walk and returned at 9:45 pm. Sometimes reading makes me tired, so I tried that, with no success.

I went up to bed, and my wife and I talked about Ground Zero and other the events of the day, including Brendan's day at college and Christian's day at grade school. When I think of my two children, I feel nothing but pride in them and their lives. This seemed to relax me, and after about an hour, I fell asleep knowing how terrific my kids are and how lucky I am to have them.

At 1:30 a.m. I awakened out of a sound sleep by a banging on the front door of my house. I jumped up and immediately thought about the employee I had fired the week before for stealing from my tool shed. Originally from French Guyana, he spoke with a thick accent that at times was incomprehensible. He had called me countless times in the past few days asking for his job back, but I refused. I couldn't take a chance with him stealing from my customers, so hiring him back was not plausible. Besides, I was still quite angry with him.

I ran down the stairs with Christian right behind me. The loud banging had also awakened him. Keep in mind; I was wearing only my underwear.

I ripped open the front door and yelled out, "I'm going to kick your ass." Standing on my front porch was my next-door neighbor, Christine. She appeared to be in a state of panic and said, "Jon, the house is on fire."

"Which house?" She pointed to her house.

I turned to Christian. "Get Mommy up and out of the house."

I ran outside with Christine, still in nothing but my underwear, and she pointed to where the fire was. I told her to stay out of the burning house and that I would be right back. I ran back into my house, put on shorts and a tee shirt and ran back out. Dorothy and Christian were right behind me when I told them it was the neighbor's house. They went back inside to call 911.

When I got to the front door of the burning house, I asked Christine, "Where's George?"

George was her live-in boyfriend. "He went back inside, she said."

I looked at her and hoped she didn't see the fear in my eyes. I told her to wait for the first fire truck to arrive and tell whoever it was that I was inside the burning house. I would be doing a primary search on the second floor where the fire was.

When I entered the house through the front door, flames were coming from all the windows on the front of the house. I thought to myself if George is in there and trapped, he's dead.

I made my way through the living room to the stairway at the center of the house. By now the smoke had worked its way down to the first floor, and I was crawling on my stomach, choking from the smoke. I inched my way up the stairs coughing and gagging. The stench made me nauseous but I kept going up. When I got to the top, my face was on the floor because of the smoke. I raised my head and saw everything in the two rooms on fire. The fire was intensely hot due to the aluminum siding on the house that kept the heat in. I worked my way about fifteen feet inside the first room where the fire had started. Not a sign of George. I started yelling "George, where are you?"

No answer.

I crawled a little further into the burning room. My arms were starting to feel the heat, something like a bad sunburn. I kept yelling for George, but still no answer. I realized it was becoming way too hot and dangerous for me to still be in there.

I yelled one last time, "George, we have to get out, I'm cooking in here." I started working my way back to the stairway and yelled for him one last time.

Again, nothing.

I crawled down the stairs headfirst and again thought if George was still up there, he was finished. I got to the bottom of the stairs and Mike Escobar, my neighbor from across the street, came running in.

He grabbed me, pulled me off the staircase, and asked, "Are you alright?"

"Yes," I said, "now get the hell out of this house."

" Not without you," he replied.

We both crawled out and when we got down off the front porch, we saw George across the street. George had gone to another neighbor's house to call 911. God Dammit, I was glad to see him. I've seen countless people killed in fires over the years, but never my next-door neighbor, and I didn't want to start now. A tremendous sense of relief came over me. No one was going to die this day.

Later on, I told Mike Escobar how dangerous it was for him to run into the house because he had no firefighting training. I also told him how much I appreciated the fact he put his life on the line for me, but that he shouldn't make it a habit.

I went to my work truck and put on my fire gear, and when the first truck pulled up, I hit the hydrant, and their men made their way in and extinguished the fire. Although the volume of fire was large, it was put out with relative ease.

On a firefighting level, the Freeport Fire Department is head and shoulders above the rest.

After the fire was knocked down, I went back inside to survey the damage. George told me there was money in a dish in the living room on a table and he needed to retrieve it. I told him I would go and look. When I got up there, everything that had been in the living room had been thrown out of the windows during the overhaul operations. I went down to tell George, and when I returned to the second floor, I was taken aback by what I saw and heard.

While ascending the stairway to the second floor, I heard several firefighters commenting on the remaining contents of the living room. I heard one firefighter say, "Look at the way this place is done up, are they devil worshipers?"

Another firefighter yelled, "They must be, they live next to Jon Wright, don't they?" Apparently they did not realize we were nearing Halloween, nor that I had heard everything they'd said.

I stayed silent and stood at the front of the stairway and watched these two pitiful excuses for firefighters intentionally break the remaining furniture.

" What the fuck are you doing?" I asked angrily. "There's no reason to break all of that stuff up."

They said nothing. They'd been caught vandalizing property and making disparaging remarks about another firefighter from another company. What could their motives possibly be? Assistant Chief John Maguire walked in and ordered me out of the house. I looked him dead in the eye and told him what was going on, and said he had better do something about it. I also asked, "What if the newspapers got wind of this?"

"Get out right now or you are suspended," he said.

I walked out in complete disbelief thinking, what is going on here? Why would the chief allow this to happen? Why would the chief order me, an experienced firefighter, out of the house?

I was about to lose my temper when Bill McBride, the lieutenant in from my company arrived at the scene, came over to me and asked if I was okay. I was coughing and had vomited from all the smoke I had inhaled. I walked over to the truck, took some oxygen and felt better after a few minutes.

Then I told McBride what had just transpired in the fire building. He said he would look into it. Bill is a Lieutenant in the NYPD and a professional supervisor. I had faith in Bill that he'd get to the bottom of it, but I was not prepared to wait. I marched my ass right over to Assistant Chief Maguire and told him I wanted to talk to him either here at the scene after all units had secured, or at the firehouse later on. I told him we had issues to resolve and that it was better handled now than later. I told him I was pissed off, and that one way or the other, he'd better deal with it. He gave me condescending 'I am the chief' look and walked away.

I again thought, Who are these two firefighters and who do they think they are? Why didn't Assistant Chief Maguire discipline those two firefighters immediately? Why are they still inside the house and me outside? I was going to get answers and not keep quiet about this. The chief was flexing his Chief muscles. David Bowie sang about a man "Making love with his ego," and there it was, right in front of my eyes.

Dorothy and Christian had gone back to our house after providing water for all the firefighters. They tried to go back to sleep, but because of all the noise, found sleep impossible. I went home after the last fire truck left and took another shower. I also tried to go to sleep, but my adrenaline was still flowing.

I walked over to my wife and told her what had happened. She was first astonished then angry. I asked her to keep quiet and that I would handle it. I decided not to tell George, Christine, and of course Eric, who owned the house. This would have made a difficult situation worse.

Within the next two hours, the fire marshal showed up and the house board-up crew arrived. When the crew started boarding the windows, I decided it was time to have a talk with Assistant Chief Maguire. I had approached him three times previously and each time, he said, "Not now, I'm busy." My patience was gone, and when I approached him for the final time, he walked briskly to his chief's car, got in, and drove away.

This was a sign of things to come. My relationship with him has deteriorated drastically since then, and he has become choleric to my fire company and me. To date, neither of the firefighters who did the damage and made the remarks about me have been disciplined. This is just another example of the double standard that exists.

Fire chiefs are elected in the volunteer fire service, not appointed due to qualifications. It makes me scratch my head in amazement. Politics always has and always will permeate and govern the fire service. I often wonder if the chief gets so offensive because he knows he's doing things in the fire service that may be construed as illegal, or that they produce the appearance of impropriety on his part. I believe his actions were cowardly.

Shortly after the chief left, Eric's mother and father arrived, and I told them what had happened. They said Eric was at his property upstate and didn't have a phone, but they knew roughly where the property was.

Given that information, I made a phone call to the New York State Police in that area, and within one hour they found him. He arrived back at the house at about 9 a.m. that morning. When told the fire started as a result of candles, he was less than happy, and let George and Christine know it.

I can certainly understand his distress and did my best to console him.

Experiencing that neighborhood fire, I thought of the frustration Otto Pulse had gone through. I was more determined than ever to get to the bottom of the problem in Massapequa. I called Otto and recounted to him what had happened to my neighbor's house. He simply said, "I told you so."

Three weeks after I'd started gathering information for Otto, I found a note on the dashboard of my work truck and on the note was a message: Stay away from 11758. That's the zip code for Massapequa, NY.

I called the police and they took a Suspicious Incident Report. Two weeks after that, I found a rock on the hood of my truck and the windshield broken. Two months after that, I had a disturbing phone call from a man who identified himself at Steven Zimmerman. The telephone conversation went something like this:

" Hello."

" Is Jonathan Wright there?"

" This is he."

Steven Zimmerman said, "Stay out of Massapequa, it is none of your business."

"Who is this again?"

"Steven Zimmerman, chief of the Massapequa Fire Department, and what we do is none of your concern."

"This is all a matter of public record, and I am entitled to it."

" If you come back to Massapequa again, there is going to be trouble."

" I will be there tomorrow."

He hung up the phone.

I called the Freeport Police department and made a formal complaint. It turns out Steven Zimmerman is not only the chief of the Massapequa Fire Department, he is also a New York City police detective.

The next day, I lodged a formal complaint with the New York City Bureau of Internal Affairs. I spoke to internal affairs on two separate occasions, and they assured me this would never happen again.

After being stonewalled by the Nassau County Police Department, Otto and I decided to lay low for a while to see what would happen next. We were not surprised. Otto's business was broken into three times subsequent to the incident with Steven Zimmerman.

To date, the police department had not solved the arson at Otto Pulse's building.

~~

In my job I have come to know some very astute firefighters. My dear friend Vinnie Segreto, a retired New York City firefighter and very knowledgeable in almost all aspects of fire suppression, later helped me theorize the collapse of the towers. He explained that steel relaxes and begins to fail at 1400 degrees Fahrenheit and melts at 2800 degrees Fahrenheit. The initial crash and explosion into the towers created heat in excess of 3200 degrees Fahrenheit, thus the collapse. The piece of steel I was looking at probably came from the area of the explosion.

Vinnie helped me realize that anyone who was on those floors when the planes hit was vaporized instantly. The human body is consumed at 1600 degrees Fahrenheit. I take solace knowing that many of my friends never knew what hit them when they perished. They died instantly.

The rather large chunk of steel that looked like a radiator was in reality a piece of the steel frame that had been exposed to the initial crash, explosion and fire that followed the initial attack.

We continued working on the pile in futility. With Charlie being my safetyman on the other end of the lifeline we were now using, I popped out of a hole and looked over about one hundred feet to my left. There was a small pile in comparison to the larger piles, about the size of my house, and through the massive steel and burning material I could see a glow at the center of the pile.

"If anyone is in there, they've been cremated," I said to Charlie.

"You got that right."

"Can you feel the radiant heat coming from that pile?"

"Got any marshmallows?" he said, making light of the moment. It was what we had to do in order to keep on with our work.

I laughed all the way back into the hole and continued my search. When I got about ten feet inside the pile, my eyes stopped burning. For some reason the air inside the pile didn't bother me as much as when I was on the surface.

I continued talking to Charlie until I heard that descriptive "shhhhhhhh", and "quiet" coming from everyone on the pile. I worked my way out, and Charlie told me someone had heard what sounded like a tapping on a beam.

A search and rescue team from Missouri came to the base of the pile I was working on. They carried a telescoping camera that could be projected twenty feet inside a pile of debris. Charlie and I watched as they advanced the camera inside the pile.

I could hear people twenty feet away from me breathing.

It was silent for about ten minutes until this team realized the noise was indistinguishable.

I took a breather and went to the bottom of the pile where I struck up a conversation with the woman who operated the camera. Her name was Patti, and she came from the Kansas City Fire Department. She had arrived that morning and told me she and two of the firefighters with her had also been in Okalahoma City after the bombing of the Alfred Murrah Federal Building in 1995. I asked her to equate the two events and she said Oklahoma City paled in comparison. Our conversation ended quickly, as she and her crew were soon called to another part of the scene. While walking away, she said, "Be careful, Freeport."

I will probably never see her again but it doesn't matter. We were all together in this mess, trying desperately to make sense out of it.

I'm still trying.

# Wright family firefighter history

Emory Wright (kneeling) and Freeport
Second Battalion.

Emory Wright (center) and
"The Silk Stocking Gang" at
Second Battalion Tournament,
Freeport, NY, Sept. 7, 1947.

## Five

### Randy, Dad, & Pop

I stood twenty-five feet above the pile next to where the FDNY had found the ladder truck with six dead firefighters on board. Climbing out of the pile was a firefighter who was not very tall. I watched as he laboriously worked his way over to the ladder truck that had been brought in to try and put water on the ever-burning fires.

At the ladder truck, after a brief discussion with the duty lieutenant, he ascended the aerial ladder, which had been extended about sixty feet at a forty-five degree angle. He climbed the ladder like a monkey climbing through vines.

When he got to the top, he signaled remotely to lower the ladder, and with a pike pole he tried pulling things off the pile beneath him where the fires were burning.

Given the circumstances, I found this amazing This firefighter was as agile a man as I have ever seen. I have experience climbing, so I appreciated his talent. He reminded me of my father when I was a young boy . . .

~~

On a Sunday morning my dad, brother Randy and I were in the back yard on Smith Street helping my dad with the lawn. My godfather, former Chief Bob Kinsey was sitting on a chair reading his paper and chomping on his ever-present cigar. We lived in a duplex two-family house on Smith Street, and Uncle Bob lived right next door. My mother was in the kitchen making breakfast for us 'working men.' We could see her through the window that overlooked the back yard. In the faint distance, we heard the fire whistle begin with the siren following. That meant only one thing – an all-out sprint to the firehouse. My brother Randy stayed behind while my father and I bolted to the firehouse three blocks away. We ran west on Smith Street to Church Street, turned left and ran two more blocks to the firehouse.

My dad would often let me get there first so I could open the firehouse doors and let the truck out. Smokey, the firehouse Dalmatian, usually greeted us.

Smokey was a fairly large dog, and when the fire calls sounded, he jumped on the truck and waited for firemen to arrive. There was only one problem. After the call, when the fire truck returned to the firehouse, Smokey wouldn't let anyone get off the truck! He would growl, snarl, and occasionally nip at anyone who tried.

As you might imagine, this became a big problem. As time went on, Smokey took to going after people walking past the firehouse. Which would be a dangerous thing, indeed. Eventually Smokey had to be kept on a leash, and after he chewed his way out of the leash and bit someone, he was suddenly gone. They didn't have the heart to tell me what happened to old Smokey until many years later

As was their custom after a call, the firefighters would sit at the table and critique what happened at the call. That day was no different. The fire was a small kitchen fire and had been put out quickly without incident.

We gathered at the round table near the back of the apparatus floor in Truck Company's firehouse. I was only eight or nine years old at the time and sat in awe of these firefighters. The guys talked about their firefighter tournament team. It went on to take the state point trophy that year at the state tournament in Syracuse, NY. The original name of the tournament team was the Silk Stocking Gang, and got its name from the firemen who first started

Excelsior Hook and Ladder Company #1 in the late 1800's.

Back then, Truck Company, as it is now known, was organized by several local businessmen and civic leaders. The nickname came from the firemen who were often dressed in suits and ties and always wore silk stockings. As time evolved, the stigma relaxed and the team changed its name to The Dead End Kids.

As I sat on the floor watching, along with my father at the table were Bruce Willets, Don Mauersberger, Norman Schmeling, Don Effinger, Don Reilly, Vinnie Segreto and sometimes, my grandfather, Pop Wright. On Sunday mornings we'd go to the firehouse and then off to the tournament field for tournament practice.

When we got to Fireman's Field on Sunrise Highway, I'd help unload tournament equipment off the fire truck. There were buckets for the bucket brigade, fittings for the all the hose couplings, the throwing ladder for the ladder events and the hose and ladder carts.

After we got the equipment off the aerial ladder, the team would always practice ladder events first. These were my favorite because my father was the principal ladder climber, and I was always watching and amazed at how fast he climbed.

The one-man ladder team would set up at the start line, team captain Don Mauersberger Sr. would call the start, and off they went. I watched them down the track to the line where they'd pull the ladder off the cart and throw it in the air. The top of the ladder would hit the tournament arch. At the same time the ladder is being thrown through the air, the climber, my father, would launch himself through the air, grab the ninth rung of the ladder while it was still moving, and start climbing to the top.

Most times, he would reach the top of the ladder just as it hit the top of the arch. My father stands only five feet three inches tall. He jumped almost ten feet off the ground to climb that ladder.

The ladder events were my favorite because my father was the star of the team. To this day, I have never seen anyone climb as well as my father, and I have often tried . . .

~~

I watched the FDNY firefighter at Ground Zero on the ladder attempting to move some debris from a section of the pile that had been burning for days. He seemed frustrated that he was unable to move one of the smaller steel beams with his pike pole. He descended the ladder down to the firefighter on the turntable of the aerial ladder, who handed him a pick-head axe.

I think he was trying to untangle some of the steel reinforcement rods that were twisted like pretzels in the massive pile. They were intertwined with broken bits of concrete that had survived being pulverized in the collapse. Some of the other firefighters were pointing to a mark on one of the steel beams that indicated where a body might be.

I maneuvered my way about fifty yards to my right to get a better look at what was written on the steel beam. Then I stopped dead in my tracks. On the large steel beam above the firefighter, written in big, bold, neon orange letters was 'BODY DOWN HERE TWENTY FEET' with an arrow pointing down.

It was ominous. Creepy.

The firefighter, who was now back atop the aerial ladder, started reaching with his axe to untangle some of the steel reinforcement rods. He wasn't having much success, and I heard him yell down to drop the aerial ladder down ten feet to where he could climb down onto the large steel beam.

The steel beam was at an approximate forty-five degree angle and made the steel reinforcement rods more accessible. After the ladder came down, the firefighter jumped off the ladder onto the steel beam. I thought this was either incredibly brave of incredibly stupid.

After watching him for several minutes, I realized there was no way he was going to be able to free up the steel reinforcement rods from the pile. The steel beam he was standing on was about eight feet wide and twenty-five feet tall on the forty-five degree angle. All of a sudden, the firefighter slipped and started to slide down the steel beam towards the burning pile. I thought to myself, this man is dead. He will be incinerated. Just as I said that to Charlie, the firefighter did something my father taught me to do as a young man in the construction business. He lay down flat on the beam and . . .

~~

July 17, 1971.

The sun was bright, the day was warm and the birds were chirping. I was working with my dad on a roof job on Lena Avenue in Freeport.

We'd started this roof job three days before and were going to finish either today or tomorrow. The house was an old Queen Anne style with many valleys, very high, and abnormally steep. We had scaffolding set up in the upper rear section and my dad and Joe Bachety, a retired Freeport Police officer, were working up on the roof. It was time to break for lunch so they came down, and off we went to Kelly's for burgers. Kelly's was in the middle of town on Merrick Road, about one block from the firehouse.

As we ordered, my older brother Randy, who had just graduated from Freeport High School, met us. My dad told us about some of the fires he had been to with my grandfather.

Like the time the fireman from Hose 3 fell off the fire truck on the way to a call. The guy ended up in the hospital with a broken neck, but he survived with no paralysis. My dad said he was lucky to be alive.

Dad turned to me and asked what I would do if all of a sudden I started to fall or slide down a roof. I told him I would grab for anything I could get my hands on.

He looked at me and simply said, "Wrong answer."

"What are you talking about?" I asked baffled.

"If you never remember anything else I ever tell you, remember this …," he paused and looked intently in my eyes.

"Remember what?"

"If you lose you balance, if you slip, or if you start falling down the roof, or if the roof gives out under you, SPREAD EAGLE," he instructed.

I gave him a dumbfounded look like he was a certifiable nut. He went on to explain to me that in order not to slide down off the roof, you need friction. Spreading eagle is exactly that. "You spread your arms and legs as far apart as you possibly can," he explained. "The friction will stop you from going over, and it will save your life."

He had no smile on his face. I could tell he was deadly serious. Joe and my brother both looked at me and said in unison, "Listen to dad."

Reluctantly, I agreed, we finished our lunches, and went back to the job.

When we got back there, Dad told me to bring up shingles to the top section where the scaffold was. Each bundle of shingles weighed over eighty pounds, and I had to carry them up the ladder forty feet to the bottom section of the scaffold. I decided I would quickly carry ten bundles up the ladder and place them on the bottom section before they got their tools on and climbed up. I was going to impress them with my young speed and climbing ability.

After getting the shingles up to the bottom section, I had to move them up two more sections to the top. I moved all ten bundles to the middle section, which was fifteen feet from the bottom of the roof.

I moved myself to the middle section and started moving the shingles up to the top. With no warning, the middle section of scaffolding gave way. I was now sliding upside down on my back with my head toward the bottom edge of the roof. All I could thing of was SPREAD EAGLE.

I spread my arms and legs as far as I could, but I kept sliding, although considerably slower. When I reached the bottom edge of the roof, I almost stopped, my hands caught the rain gutter, and then I stopped completely. I screamed as loud as I could for help and within seconds, my dad was up the ladder grabbing me so I wouldn't fall off. Had I fallen, I am certain I would have been killed. Joe threw the other ladder on the other side of me and climbed up, grabbed me, and helped me flip over. I managed to get my foot on the bottom section of scaffolding and pulled myself up onto it.

I sat on the remaining lower scaffolding shaking uncontrollably and started to hyperventilate. I must have used every curse in the book. On the verge of panic, my dad grabbed me by the neck, turned me and stared me dead in the eyes where tears had welled up, and he said, "You're okay; take a deep breath."

"What the hell happened?"

"The middle scaffolding plank broke when you dropped the last bundle of shingles on it," he said. "There was no way any of us could have known that plank would break. It was almost new." After ten minutes, my shaking stopped. I calmed down, and went down the ladder. I found the garden hose and rinsed my head off before I headed home for the day – or so I thought.

My dad looked over at me. "Where are you going?"

" Home," I said.

"Not yet you're not!"

I was startled. "Why not?"

He explained to me that I had just nearly been killed and that if I didn't go right back up that ladder, I might never be able to climb again.

Suffice it to say, I thought of it as falling off a horse and getting right back on. I started climbing the ladder and immediately started shaking. I turned and looked at my dad.

"Keep going," he yelled.

I stopped for a few seconds, and then continued up the ladder. I reached the top, then started back down.

"Don't come down here until you get off the ladder onto the scaffolding," he said at the top of his lungs.

"Are you crazy?" I screamed back at him.

He screamed right back, "Maybe so." Then he shook the ladder.

I froze for a few seconds, and then he yelled up to me, "You can't come down until you get off the ladder onto the scaffolding."

That's when I got mad. I jumped off the ladder and yelled down to him, "Are you fucking satisfied?"

"Yes," he calmly replied.

I was still shaking when I got to the bottom, and said nothing as I walked past him and went home. My father saved my life on July 17, 1971 . . .

~~

SPREAD EAGLE! The technique I was watching the fireman perform as he slid down the steel beam was a part of the trade. Luckily, he came to a stop after about ten feet.

He was face down with his feet pointed downward. The steel beam was covered with the same dust that engulfed the entire area. It must have seemed like snow on a ski slope. It looked like a nuclear winter. I know what that firefighter was thinking and feeling when he slid down toward the burning inferno below. He most certainly might have been killed.

Firefighters from all around scrambled to get over to him and help him off the steel beam. The aerial ladder operator dropped the ladder down and picked up the imperiled firefighter. It was not his time to die.

Charlie and I worked our way back up the pile to where we were before the incident with the firefighter on the aerial ladder. While we made our way up, a couple of ironworkers were making their way up the pile as well. They were using torches to cut away all the twisted and mangled steel beams away from where bodies might be found and to make the way safe for rescue workers.

One of the problems they experienced was getting the large bottles of acetylene and oxygen up to where the steel needed to be cut away. On one occasion, we helped them carry the bottles up onto the pile in Stokes baskets. Stokes baskets are used in the fire service to move a patient, or in this case, recovered bodies from the scene. The Stokes baskets held exactly two bottles. Every time we brought up two bottles of gas, the Stokes basket came down with either a body or body parts. We were in Hell.

When Charlie and I returned to our original position, we started removing the seemingly endless supply of crushed debris. Very little debris was intact due to the collapse, and the parts that remained were unrecognizable.

Some replacements from the FDNY had arrived and were taking their places on the pile. One of their men struck a remarkable resemblance to one of my former friends Ralph Smith.

Ralph was a former trustee of the Village of Freeport and a former member of the Freeport Fire Department. Ralph was a nice man with whom I used to be friends. But over time, because of a trophy that was in the trophy case at Hose 1 on Southside Avenue in Freeport, our relationship had suffered irreparable damage . . .

~~

The trophy had been in the trophy case for more than fifty years and was given to Hose 1 as a measure of thanks to the community. The KKK awarded the trophy to Hose 1. That's right, the Ku Klux Klan. In the late 1930s 40s, the KKK was influential in the Village of Freeport. History teaches that the KKK hated anyone who wasn't white Anglo Saxon Protestant. That included Catholics, Jews, Asian,

Hispanics, and just about anyone else who didn't fit their acceptable profile. The Freeport Fire Department had participated in some point parades and tournaments that year, and the KKK thought it appropriate to make a gesture of thanks.

The trophy sat in the trophy case for fifty years until someone decided that it was racist and should be removed.

My grandfather George Wright, who didn't have a racist bone in his body, was a charter member of Hose 1, and was part of the tournament team. But at the time Village trustee, Ralph Smith, insinuated that anyone who had anything to do with the tournament team, and accepted the trophy from the KKK, including my grandfather, was a racist. Ralph took his accusations not only to the village board and the mayor, but also to the newspapers. This was front-page news for several weeks.

I was accosted by several people at a meeting in village hall in Freeport over this matter, and I was also dubbed racist.

For the record, my best friend is Chinese and to call me a racist is absurd. I experienced the race riots at Freeport High School during the late 1960s and early 70s. I know what it's like to be victimized if only by circumstances. This historical episode in the Village of Freeport is a reminder of how inept politics can be as result of the personal biases of the people involved. No one has had the decency to broach the subject with me. I cannot stand idly by while others disparage my family name with lies, innuendo, and false statements . . .

~~

Another hour working on the pile had passed and I made my way back to the heavy rescue truck to find some food. When we were at the staging area directly beneath the Manhattan Bridge, trailers had been assembled to give supplies to the firefighters involved in the search and rescue operations at Ground Zero. Chief Wensley told us to get something to eat at that time because he didn't know when we would eat again. By now I was famished and anything was appealing. Filthy, exhausted and hungry. Ready to eat, to say the least.

Lt. Tucker managed to smuggle chips, boxes of donuts and an assortment of junk food into the back of the heavy rescue truck without telling anyone.

What a great surprise! When we finished, we knew we would return to the pile and relieve some of the FDNY firefighters. This time though, we didn't have to go far. Remember, the front bumper of our rescue truck was parked directly over the curb of the circular driveway that once connected Tower One and Tower Two of the World Trade Center. Now it was just rubble and the pile sloped upward from the front of our truck and crested in my estimation, three hundred feet in front of us, and rose about one hundred fifty feet.

While digging through the rubble at the front of the truck, I found some tourist pamphlets about the Towers. I remembered five years earlier when my wife, Dorothy, son, Christian, and my in-laws, Roger and Janet, went into Manhattan to sightsee and visit the World Trade Center. On that particular day, Christian's stroller fell apart on one of the cobblestone streets, and Roger had to carry Christian for the rest of the day. They went to the top of Tower One, and for many days they talked about the view. I remembered all of this, and I have nightmares now about what might have happened had my family been up there during the attacks, and I still have the pamphlets. My wife refuses to look at them and has not gone back to Manhattan since September 11.

Lt. Tucker and I stopped our work long enough to share a drink of water with a New York City police. Wally, along with another police officer and firefighter, helped us to clear away the deformed steel reinforcement rods that littered the area directly in front of the heavy rescue truck. We stopped and talked for a few minutes until there was a disturbance about fifty feet away from us up on the pile.

One of the firefighters from the FDNY was arguing with battalion Chief DeMarco about moving his position to another spot. There was an ironworker who wanted to cut a beam and the firefighter was in the way. "I'm not moving, I'm going to find Chucky," he screamed.

Chief DeMarco told him he was relieved and ordered him down off the pile. He left – reluctantly. Chief Wensley, who was at the command post, and I just looked at each other. I immediately smiled at him, he smiled at me, and we continued on with the task at hand . . .

~~

Chief Wensley and I had a deep understanding of the situation. On November 11, 1999, Bill McBride, Kathleen Stoessel, and I had taken the heavy rescue truck out for driver's practice.

While we were out, we headed toward the diner on Merrick Road to get some food. I went inside and ordered, waited, then took the food out to the truck. We prepared to leave.

As I boarded the truck, we heard over the radio that the police were sending a car to Merrick Road and Park Avenue, about one mile down the road for an accident. Bill and I agreed we could probably get there before the police.

We arrived at the scene at the same time as the police officer. I was the officer in charge, so it was my responsibility to size up the situation and make a report to the incoming chief, who happened to be John Wensley.

I found an overturned car leaning on high voltage wires with victims trapped inside. My immediate consideration was the safety of my fellow firefighters and myself. Because we were on driver's practice, we didn't have fire gear with us. I ordered Bill and Kathleen to stabilize the vehicle while I attempted to open the doors. Jimmy Olin, the Chief of the department, had also arrived at the scene, and he assisted in trying the dented doors. We were unable to open them. By now, third assistant Chief Wensley arrived at the scene and came up to me and ordered me to step back and let the men with gear do the work.

It was the correct thing to do under normal circumstances. These, however, were not normal circumstances. These victims' lives were in immediate danger due to the high voltage wires, and one of them was unconscious. We had to get them out as quickly as possible.

I am a certified New York State EMT/CC, which means I am an Advanced Life Support provider and the senior ranking medical authority at the scene. Given the circumstances, I felt it was my duty to continue trying to extricate the victims. Dutifully, I ignored Chief Wensley's order and continued on. No one on scene had full gear, and nobody outranked me medically, so I felt his order was not warranted. But he was intent on keeping me out of the way.

He grabbed my arm, turned me around and told me if I didn't get back, I would be suspended immediately. I told him in no uncertain terms to keep his hands off me, and then I stepped back. I thought to myself I would handle the problem after the injured were taken care of.

After the call, he came up to me and suspended me. I thought to myself, the newest chief is only trying to flex his chief muscles.

When we returned to the firehouse, I slipped getting off the truck and hurt my back. The chief was notified. I received a suspension letter and called for a special meeting, setting the scene for a showdown.

The fire council meeting is held on the third Tuesday of each month, which was only one week away. Because of my injury, I requested an adjournment and it was granted.

They continued the suspension for another month,

during which I was not allowed to answer any calls. I called Chief Wensley on the phone and asked him to come over to my house to talk about all of this. I had decided it was not worth pursuing and that if he agreed, my suspension would be for time served.

When he came to my house, he was less than graceful. Trying to be persuasive, he was loud and boisterous. He was in my house so this behavior was insulting, like it didn't matter who was right or wrong, he was the chief and that's that. After fifteen minutes of his diatribe, I told him enough was enough and to leave my house. He walked out in a huff, and I told him I would see him at the hearing.

Prior to the hearing, I sent a letter to the secretary of the fire council, Tony Fiore. In this letter I requested specific information critical to my defense. My thinking was simple. I had to discredit the chief and his actions. Because of the political make up of the Freeport Fire Department; I decided the best way to do this was to bring into question his qualifications as chief. I requested copies of all his qualifications including any qualifying certificates, awards, training logs, etc.

The day of the hearing arrived, and I still had not received the information I was entitled to. Knowing I could not proceed with my defense, I requested another adjournment until such time as I was provided with the information. I simply would not proceed until I was prepared.

At 10 p.m. that night, I got a phone call from Lt. John McGuire. He told me that the fire council had the hearing without me being there, upheld the suspension, and kept it as time served, just like I had proposed to Chief Wensley.

I wondered how they could hold a hearing without me in attendance. Then I realized why they did it. They had never before had anyone challenge the way they did things. They'd never had anyone stand up to them in this manner. They never had anyone question a chief's qualifications publicly. It is not common knowledge, but the fire council and any disciplinary hearings are public meetings. Anyone can attend, watch, ask questions, and listen to this three-ring circus. The Freeport Fire Department was not about to let any of this become public.

That's just what happened back in the early 60s when my father was a member of the new truck committee for Truck Company. He, along with his best friend Bruce Willets, made up the core of the committee. The others were Whitey and John Boland, Freddie Frankel, Norman Schmeling, Don Mauersberger Sr., Bob Ahrens, and Paul Perez. As was their custom, they would go to the Seagrave fire truck factory to inspect the progress on the new truck during the course of its construction. This is the way it has been done for decades and the way it is done today. As in all organizations, groups form that sometimes disagree with each other. The fire department is no different.

At this particular time, a visit to the factory in Columbus, Ohio was scheduled. The chairman of the committee was Don Mauersberger Sr. Apparently he wanted to have total control over the committee and decide who would go to the factory. He elected himself, Freddie Frankel and Norman Schmeling, effectively blocking any input the others might have.

My father was an important member of the committee because of his original design to have the tiller of the aerial ladder enclosed. This had never been done before and was an eye opener. Mauersberger and others were against it, and they tried to prevent my father and Bruce Willets from going to the factory. When my dad got wind of what he was trying to do, he contacted the fire chief at the time, Frank Musso, and asked if he and Bruce could use the chief's car to drive to Ohio and inspect the new truck.

Chief Musso agreed and gave the car to my dad. They arrived in Ohio, went to the hotel where the others were staying who had flown in and checked in. My dad learned where they were eating dinner and told me that when he and Bruce walked in, Mauersberger and his company were speechless and angry. My dad, after driving for twelve hours, wasn't even given the courtesy of having dinner with Mauersberger. He was ignored. It is fair to say this would not be the end of it.

At the next regular company meeting of Truck Company, Mauersberger made a ruckus about my father spending company money to go Ohio. After another long verbal battle, a vote was taken and the company approved what my dad had done. After he won the vote, he went to the front of the room and handed Captain Paul Perez, one hundred dollars the company had seen fit to give him in the first place.

Dad felt his honor had been questioned, therefore he refused to take what others may have felt was tainted money. He gave the money back and kept his honor. The others didn't. Their attempt to discredit my dad and Bruce was thwarted, and they looked stupid doing it, but the damage to their reputations had been done.

Bruce Willets had been my dad's best friend for most of their lives. He was Captain of Truck Company in 1951-1952. My dad was Captain 1950-1951. Bruce decided that the nonsense going on was too much, and he told my dad he was going to transfer to Rescue Company. My father, loyal and true to form, joined him. They are best friends still . . .

~~

Back on the pile at Ground Zero, Chief DeMarco convinced the angry firefighter to move away from the pile, and the search continued without incident. Chief Wensley and I just smiled at each other again and we continued on with our grim task. Since the time of my incident with Wensley, he and I had a new rapport and a new found respect for each other. Especially after entering Ground Zero. We were both profoundly affected by what we saw, and I think we realized these differences didn't matter anymore.

Six

# My Firsts

CAPTAIN Bentley, Lt. Tucker, and I stood at the front of the heavy rescue truck watching the infinite supply of five-gallon pails pass us on bucket lines. We were amazed at how many pails there were. Occasionally, a red pail would pass us signifying a body part was inside. Most times, red bags visually stated the obvious. When that happened, people stood at silent attention and paid their respects.

In one of the passing buckets, I caught a glimpse of the contents. It looked so incredibly like a baby, I did a double take, as did Captain Bentley and Lt. Tucker. My heart pounded when I walked over to the pail and took a closer look inside. My first thought was this guy doesn't really know what he is carrying. I was prepared for the worst. It was bad enough dealing with all the dead bodies and body parts; did I really have to experience a dead baby? It wouldn't be the first time, but it would be the most horrifying. Babies are innocent; you never get used to seeing anything like that.

I could barely breathe as I looked into the pail and then looked at the others with a sigh of relief. Dave and I both have children and I don't know how badly I would have reacted had it been a baby's body or body part. Thank God I didn't have to find out. I looked to the heavens and gave thanks, and took a deep breath.

Chief Wensley and Chief DeMarco walked through a pile of debris to get to us and when they arrived, I told them about the bucket incident. Chief DeMarco commented that nothing would surprise him anymore. Chief Wensley agreed, glanced into the bucket, and asked, "Where are your gloves?"

I told him my hands were like leather because of my real job, and that I wasn't worried about them getting cut from all the rough metal edges. He looked at me and said, "Don't make me order you to wear gloves."

"Don't worry chief, I'll be fine," I answered.

"NOW!" he retorted.

Rebelliously, I complied. I didn't say a word. I just pulled my gloves out of my pocket, glared at Chief Wensley, put them on, and displayed my hands to him. By now there was quite a commotion resulting from the "baby bucket". Others had congregated and most had the same horrified look when they looked in the bucket. Most also had the same look of relief after they realized it was a doll.

Captain Bentley and I decided to join a bucket line. We had been on top of and inside the pile for almost twenty-four hours and by now, were tiring. Our eyes were constantly watering, our noses ran, and sweat poured off our brows. We were drenched from head to toe with our own sweat. Ex-Chief Julie Ellison from Hose 1 and the FDNY walked up and told me to stop crying. I must have looked terrible. It didn't matter. I was there to do a job and until I was relieved, I kept moving.

Back to the line I went. I started a conversation with Tony, the firefighter from Brooklyn, and we started trading war stories. I guess the baby in the bucket incident got him to thinking, and he asked me about the first baby I delivered . . .

~~

June, 1973. The ambulance call sounded like a bass saxophone holding a note for thirty seconds. It was a long, slow, up and down siren that could be heard for miles. Back then we didn't have pagers. We relied solely on the sirens. Dad and I decided we needed a break from the searing heat.

We jumped in the truck and responded to the firehouse.

We came from the south end of town, and when we arrived, no one else was there. We listened to the police radio, but heard nothing. After about ten minutes, we responded to the call, which was only three blocks from the firehouse. My dad, one of the first paramedics in Nassau County, told me to stay by the ambulance as he went inside. Five minutes later, he stuck his head out of the front door of the apartment, and told me to get the stretcher ready. He walked the very pregnant woman out.

She appeared to be in her early twenties and was in obvious labor pain. We placed her on the stretcher inside the ambulance. My dad told me to ride with her in the back, fill out paperwork, and try comforting her. He jumped in the driver's seat and off we went to Nassau County Medical Center.

While he was driving, he turned toward the back of the ambulance and told me to call for him if there were any problems. We drove over to Babylon Turnpike and entered the Meadowbrook Parkway northbound. Again, he said to call him if there was a problem.

As soon as he said it, the lady let out a blood-curdling holler. My dad asked what was wrong.

"I feel something," The lady yelled.

Dad asked, "Is this your first pregnancy?"

"No, it's my fifth."

Dad said, "Check if you can see anything under the blanket."

"Okay," I yelled up to him.

I looked, sat back in my seat and yelled up to dad, "You better pull over."

"Why?"

"I can see the top of the baby's head."

He had some trouble getting over to the right from the left lane, but after some evasive driving he made it. By the time he parked, walked to the back of the ambulance, and opened the door, the baby was out. I had just delivered my first baby. What a rush!

The exact date of the delivery escapes me, but the events of that day are as fresh in my mind as though it happened ten minutes ago. My father and I were installing new gutters and leaders on a house on Long Beach Avenue in Freeport. It was a hot summer day, temperature in the eighties, and quite humid. We had been working for about five hours straight.

Dad and I were reminiscing about my grandfather, Pop Wright. Pop was a tall man with a full head of white hair and usually walked slowly. He was a plumber by trade and knew how to do many things. My dad used to have Pop working with him on a regular basis doing mostly gutters and leader on houses. We talked about Pop's failing health and how even though he felt lousy, he came to work every day and kept moving. Some days he didn't accomplish very much, but I remember the look of love on my dad's face when Pop was there. It was mutual between my dad and Pop.

When Pop had came to work one day in the summer of 67, I knew something was amiss during the course of the day, but I couldn't put my finger on it. Dad was somewhat edgy and Pop was just not himself.

"I need to sit for a while," Pop yelled to dad.

"Are you all right?" Dad asked.

" Just tired," he said

I never saw my grandfather sit down for no apparent reason. It wasn't normal. I joined him, and we talked about nothing in particular. I was thankful to be with him. After about a half-hour, we went back to work, and the day ended without further event. Pop left and went home to his house in Wantagh, and Dad and I walked home across the street.

"What's wrong with Pop?" I asked.

"He's just getting old I guess." I could tell Dad was worried. After he showered, he went to see Pop. When he returned, he was painfully quiet. I asked my mom what was wrong, and she said dad was just worried about his father.

Pop died two weeks later.

Pop's funeral was a veritable plethora of firefighters from Freeport. Pop was a charter member of Hose 1 of the Freeport Fire Department, and they buried him with full fire department honors. That was the first time I ever saw my dad cry ...

~~

Back on the pile, Tony and I talked for a long time. He told me he had never delivered a baby in quite that fashion before. I told him that was my first, and we both laughed.

He started talking about the fatality his company had in a dwelling the week before and how gruesome it was. The man was burned beyond recognition. I told him I had seen that many times before, but the first time is always the worst.

~~

I'll never forget the time six people burned to death on Colonial Avenue. The house was illegally occupied when it burned and ultimately contributed to their untimely deaths.

The day before that fire, we responded to another fire on Stevens Street. Hose 5 was first to that fire and when they pulled in front of the house, flames were coming out of every window on the second floor. I was driving Hose 2 and we were second on scene.

After Hose 5 hit the hydrant, they stretched in about four hundred feet to the burning house. I hooked up to the hydrant and Truck Company passed me and positioned the aerial ladder in front of the burning house. We pulled in with four firefighters onboard and I sent them up to help Hose 5, which left me alone at the pump panel. It took fifteen minutes to get the fire knocked down, all the while; I was pumping water to Hose 5.

It was a hot summer day, and, as is normal, manpower was rare for fighting a fire. Standing about fifty feet to the east of my truck a group of teenagers started yelling obscenities at me for no apparent reason. I gave them a stern look, turned to adjust my pump, and got hit in the head with a bottle. Luckily, I have a hard head and no damage was done. Nevertheless, I was pissed off and let these punks know it. They started throwing everything in sight at me.

I grabbed the microphone for the radio and yelled for help. I told whoever was listening that I was under attack, and I needed assistance immediately. I was fighting for my life against these kids. They thought it was funny, but not me. I was scared to death. I got on the radio and called again. I heard, "Here we come."

I looked to the east and saw the cavalry running down the road. There were at least twenty firefighters, all with axes, pike poles, Halligans, and any other weapon they could muster. I was part of a fierce firefighting organization, and I knew they would always watch my back.

When the kids saw the firefighters nearing with weapons in their hands, they scattered and were not seen again.

Don Mauersberger Jr. was in the group and asked if I was all right. He noticed the bump over my right eye, and I told him I was fine. Five firefighters stayed with me at the truck until we secured. That was the first time I was attacked while fighting a fire . . .

~~

While moving the endless supply of buckets at Ground Zero, Tony and I kept talking, as talking kept our minds sharp. I asked him about his first fatality. He said he didn't remember and I told him I found that hard to believe because I will never forget my first one.

Tony was an interesting fellow. He had a wife, three kids, and his mother-in-law lived with him. He also owned a landscaping business that he ran when he was off duty. He was the American success story . . .

~~

October 1972. I was sleeping at the firehouse and my brother Randy was at home. The General Alarm of Fire was broadcast at 5:30 a.m. for a house fire at 15 Harding Place, one block from the firehouse. At the same time the alarm went off, someone knocked on the firehouse door. Kevin Vollmer answered, and the person at the door said, "The house is on fire."

"Let's go, we got a job," Kevin yelled.

We ran out to the truck and waited for a crew. Bill Sarro, "Froggy", as he is affectionately known, lived on Mount Avenue about three blocks from the firehouse. Kevin pulled the truck on the ramp and we waited for our third man so we could roll to the call. By now Chief Sonny Wallman pulled up to the scene and broadcast, "Signal 10, signal 10," in a panicky voice. Froggy pulled up and we were off to the fire. When we turned the corner, all we could see was thick, black smoke with flames shooting thirty feet in the air coming from all the front windows.

The man who had come to the firehouse walked up to Kevin and told him there was an elderly couple living in the house and that he hadn't seen them get out.

Right away, Kevin got on the radio and told the chief who was in the back yard sizing up the fire. Hose 1 was second and when they arrived, they took over the hydrant. After about ten minutes of making progress on the fire, there was still no sight of the elderly couple. The people in the neighborhood were beginning to show concern, as though some of them already knew what we were all about to find out.

I was connecting the hydrant when I heard the chief on the radio, "We have two fatalities." Suddenly every firefighter got quiet and the bystanders became somber. The neighborhood had lost its founders and everyone now knew it.

It took one half an hour to extinguish the fire and start

the overhaul. During overhaul operations, everything that
burned is thrown out of the house. This continued for an
hour.

Within that time, the police started making reports, and
the Nassau County Fire Marshal's office arrived on scene. We
started securing our truck and equipment and by the time we
were ready to leave, the police called for some firefighters to
help remove the bodies.

Kevin Vollmer, who was the captain, volunteered me to
help with the removal. I, along with my brother Randy, went
upstairs with two body bags. We were directed into the
bedroom where the bodies were and prepared the removal.
We thought if we wrapped the bodies in sheets, it would be
easier to pick them up.

Randy went to the feet and I went to the head of the
elderly gentleman. They were both burned beyond
recognition, but somehow I knew this was the man. I laid the
sheet next to the bed on the floor. Randy grabbed his legs
and I grabbed his arms. I had my firefighting gloves on and
when I went to pick him up off the burnt bed, his skin and
muscle rolled up to his biceps leaving the bones in his
forearm exposed. I dropped him, ran outside and vomited.
These were my first fatalities . . .

~~

I didn't want to think about that memory so Tony and I
continued our conversation as Captain Bentley made his way
over to us. Tony's unit was being relieved, and Dave wanted
me to ascend the pile to relieve Charlie McEneaney, who had
been digging in one spot for about two hours looking for a
body. I climbed up and told Charlie to take a break. When he
left, I watched him climb down the treacherous pile. It was
unforgiving. There were some places Charlie had to go about
one hundred feet out of his way just to descend ten feet. The
twisted steel made movement precarious at best. Every piece
we stepped on was unstable.

The slightest move in the wrong direction could be deadly. Charlie made it down in one piece, but I was concerned about his well being. I climb daily at work, so for me it was second nature. Charlie is a white-collar worker and climbing for him was challenging, but he succeeded.

Just as I got to the spot where Charlie was, I found another member of my crew, Charlie Manning. Charlie looked worse for wear, and wanted to continue, but he was spent, and soon he also climbed down.

I worked my way into the hole and started digging. For the second time in as many days, I smelled decomposing flesh. For some reason, it made me dig frantically. I was like a man possessed. The deeper I dug, the stronger the smell got, and I didn't need a cadaver-sniffing dog this time to tell me I was on the right track. I was working with a firefighter from Buffalo, NY and he felt the same way I did.

We didn't stop until we found the body about an hour later. It was the body of a male about forty years old, but was unrecognizable due to the fatal crushing injuries he sustained. His face was crushed beyond anything conceivable. We both stopped after we had the body completely uncovered, kneeled down and offered a short prayer at the same time the Stokes basket was being brought up. The Stokes basket didn't fit inside the hole so the firefighters above us handed in a backboard. It was the same kind we used for auto extrication. We wrapped the body in a sheet, placed it on a backboard, and when we did, the victim's blood poured out of his mouth. I got a knot in my stomach, felt nauseous, and once again, my heart pounded. I looked at Joe from Buffalo, and saw he was about to lose it. I told him, "Let's just get this done."

By the time we got the board out of the hole, it was covered with blood, as were we. We were about ten feet inside the pile, we added another sheet, and passed the body out. The firefighters just outside the hole placed the body in the Stokes basket, and handed it down the pile like an assembly line. It kept moving at a snail's pace down the pile, the entire time all who came in contact with it offered blessings. We were able to witness this from another hole in the tunnel we had been digging in.

Joe started out of the hole first, then I followed. The hole was barely big enough to get through. He got out and instead of climbing down, climbed up. I guess he was going to start digging someplace else. I went out stomach first and when I got out, I turned and looked up

Just as I did, Joe slipped from above me. He only fell about five or six feet, but he landed right on top of my left arm. I knew my left wrist was broken, but I wasn't about to tell anyone. Five or six firefighters came right over and asked if we were both okay. We both said yes and moved on. I didn't let on how bad it was. I told them I was going to the truck to get some air. I couldn't use my left hand for anything, but because of my climbing experience, I got down effortlessly.

When I got to the truck, a couple of FDNY firefighters asked what happened up there. I told them someone slipped and that no one was hurt. I lied. I went in the back of the truck, closed the door, and buried my head. My wrist was throbbing, my head ached, my heart was broken, and all I could think of was trying to find my brothers. We had a cooler in the back of the heavy rescue truck, which had water and ice in it. I sat next to it, opened the cooler, and buried my left arm in the ice up to my elbow.

I was able to sit there for almost half an hour before anyone came inside. As soon as the door opened, I pulled my arm out holding a bottle of water. No one knew how badly I was hurt, and I was determined to keep it that way. Lt. Tucker came in, got a bottle of water and went back out. When he left, I immersed my arm once again for about fifteen minutes. When I pulled it out, it felt much better, although I knew deep down inside it was indeed broken.

I found some white medical tape, taped my left wrist, put my fire coat and gloves on, and went back outside. I was able to keep working as long as my wrist was taped. This was the first time I ever fractured a bone in almost thirty years in the fire department.

I worked my way back up the pile to where Joe was, and he asked if I was all right. I said yes. I still had my gloves on. I stood with him while feeding in power wires for the lights that came off our heavy rescue truck. We were in a position where we had to stay put and keep feeding in wire to the men inside the pile. One of the firefighters inside the pile had found a police car with two people still in it. The firefighters inside the pile were working with the Hurst tool (Jaws of Life) and needed lighting.

Feeding in the power lines was an easy job, and I was content doing just that. Although I guess he was in his thirties, Joe was a talkative fellow who was relatively new to the fire service. He told me he was also an EMT and that he had recently had his first pre-hospital save. He asked me if I had any saves like his. I laughed. Then I told him about Paul Young . . .

~~

January 1976. Paul Young was a sixty-four-year-old who retired from his job as an engineer at Shell Oil and decided he was going to get himself into better physical condition. He joined the Freeport Recreation Center and started going to the gym every day. I had been working at the Center for about three years during the winter as a rink guard. My job was simple. Skate around and make sure everyone was safe. I had been working a lot of hours lately and looked forward to Thursdays when we got paid. This particular Thursday was no different. I drove to the Rec Center to pick up my check. While I was walking in the front door, Freeport Police officer Charlie Parker ran past me, looked back, stopped and said,

"Jon, let's go, we have a cardiac arrest in the basketball gym."

I ran behind Charlie into the gym and we found Paul Young lying face down on the gym floor. Charlie and I turned him over and checked for a pulse and breathing. There were neither. Paul Young was in full cardiac arrest. Having been trained in CPR, I started to work on him immediately. Charlie got on his portable radio and called for assistance. As soon as I started CPR, an old friend of mine from Hose 1, Dennis Eberhart came into the gym and asked if he could help. I said yes, and he began doing mouth-to-mouth while I did chest compressions. Charlie Parker went outside to get his oxygen tank and returned to the gym. Charlie, Dennis and I continued CPR until the ambulance arrived, then put Paul on the stretcher and into the ambulance. Charlie drove the ambulance to the hospital while Dennis and I continued CPR.

We performed non-stop CPR for forty-five minutes. When we got to the hospital, the emergency room staff took over, started an IV and put a breathing tube down his throat. They shocked Paul Young only once, and his heart started beating once again.

Dennis and I had had our first pre-hospital save and we were on top of the world. We got cleaned up and the ambulance driver took us back to the Rec Center.

Three days later, I got a call from Dennis and he told me Paul Young was asking for us. I wondered how he knew who we were, but it didn't matter. We had saved a life.

Dennis and I went to Lydia Hall Hospital to visit Paul. When we walked into the Coronary Care Unit, he was sitting up in bed with an oxygen mask on his face. He looked pale, but he was alive. He called us to his bedside and hugged each of us, as did his wife. I told him it was a team effort and that Police Officer Charlie Parker and the ambulance driver were equally responsible. As we were leaving, his wife followed us outside and asked for our addresses. I was uncomfortable giving my address, but Dennis was not. Three weeks later, Dennis came over and gave me a solid gold pen and pencil set bearing the logo of Shell Oil Corporation . . .

~~

Pushing more wire into the whole, Joe told me he was amazed that we were able to save Paul's life. I assured him Buffalo gets its fair share of calls and that he would undoubtedly get more opportunities. I told him to be patient. He thought I was full of crap and started ranting and raving about how quiet his firehouse was. I told him to be patient, and to be careful what you wish for, because you may just get it. Then I told him about Ivan Harris . . .

~~

September 1991. Next to Freeport Fire Headquarters is a building known as 5 Broadway. 5 Broadway is an office building that once housed the Pennysaver Corporation. Ivan Harris was the caretaker of the building and had a small apartment in the basement. He was an affable man who always said hello and occasionally came over to the firehouse and had a beer with the guys. His wife Leona didn't much care for the fire department, and didn't mind letting us know her feelings. It didn't matter. Ivan was our friend, and he knew he was always welcome.

On that sunny autumn day at the end of September, I was driving my work truck along North Main Street in Freeport. I saw Ivan standing on the corner of Leonard and Main and beeped my horn and waved. He waved back, and I continued on to my appointment.

An hour later I was leaving my customer when my fire department pager went off. We were to respond to an overturned truck at Milton and North Main Streets. I was five blocks away, and I hit the accelerator. When I got there, I saw Ivan's blue pick up truck upside down leaning against a building. I thought, "Oh my God," and ran up to the overturned truck. I held my breath hoping no one, especially

Ivan, was in the truck.

Slowly, I worked my way around a brick building to the cab of the truck. I looked inside and there was Ivan, upside down and unconscious. I yelled out to the crowd that had formed to call 911. I worked my way inside the overturned truck to where I could help Ivan. When I got into position, I tapped him on the shoulder and he was unresponsive. I checked for a pulse and breathing. He had none. I knew I had to maintain my composure otherwise the crowd would get stirred up. While I was trying to free Ivan from this crypt, I heard a siren approaching. I popped my head out and it was Assistant Chief Mike Sotira. He came right over to me. I filled in the details, and he got on his radio. Within two minutes, fire trucks and Nassau County Emergency services had arrived. I worked for the Nassau County Police Department for a while, so I knew they liked to take over a scene.

Today, this would not be the case. I didn't want anyone except my people helping Ivan. I worked frantically to free Ivan because he was choking to death. His windpipe was being crushed by the steering wheel. My company, Emergency-Rescue Company #9, was first in and went to work immediately. Because of Ivan's position within the truck, it took almost thirty minutes to extricate him. I worked on him the entire time doing CPR, starting IVs, and rescue breathing.

We finally got him out and put him in the ambulance. All the way to the hospital we did everything we knew how to do to save Ivan. We arrived at the hospital and they worked on him feverishly too, but with no success.

Ivan was pronounced dead at 3:42 p.m. This was the first friend of mine to die while under my care . . .

~~

When I finished telling Joe this story, I looked at him and could not hold back the tears. He just shook his head, said thanks, and got relieved to go home.

# A firefighter's work is never done

Jon Wright (center) and Freeport Volunteer Fire Department
at fire on Main Street, in Freeport, NY, 1996

Building fire on Church Street, in Freeport, NY, 1982-the
ladder is the first closed tiller in the U.S. and was designed by
Emory Wright and the truck design team.

Mutual Aid Call
Fire on Andrews Ave., Roosevelt, NY

Seven

# Unqualified

SUNDAY, September 16, 2001, 4 a.m. We have been at Ground Zero for over twenty-four hours and were tiring. The exhausted kind of tired that belies mere words. The type of tired that soldiers on the front line experience. It was time for a break.

For the first time since we arrived at Ground Zero, we were all at the heavy rescue truck taking a much-needed rest. Several FDNY firefighters came over to us and one by one, thanked each of us. Captain Bentley, Lt. Tucker, Charlie McEneaney, Charlie Manning, Chief Wensley, and I were all taken back by their gestures of thanks and good will.

Jimmy Butler from the FDNY, is also a Freeport Chief and he walked up to thank us as well. I've known Jimmy Butler well over forty years, and he seemed to be a little distant, but I attribute that solely to the gravity of the situation handed all of us.

As we said our good-byes to the FDNY firefighters who were being relieved, Captain Bentley tapped me on the shoulder and pointed to a group of firefighters up on the pile. Then we heard screams. "Medics, medics."

Lt. Tucker, Charlie McEneaney and I started making our way up the pile to them. We are all medically trained firefighters and knew there were no others in the vicinity. Again, we had to navigate our way through the mass of metal and concrete. Lt. Tucker and Charlie took a round about route, but I went directly to them. I was easily able to climb over the steel beams and get to the injured firefighter ahead of the others. When I got there he was surrounded by his compatriots, and I was unable to reach him. I kept trying to get in but was unable to do so. I kept thinking what if this brave firefighter is seriously injured. But the answer was simple. I had to wait. First, one of the battalion chiefs came over and looked at him, then his duty lieutenant, then another firefighter. It was endless.

Finally, out of frustration, I yelled, "I'm a medic, do you need help?" They said he had a twisted ankle and he was okay. Clearly, this was not the case, because this guy was unable to walk . . .

~~

The scene reminded me of November, 1987. I had transferred to Rescue Company from Hose 2 and had just come back from vacation. An ambulance call was transmitted for Brooklyn Avenue for a female having seizures. Charlie Naumann drove. When we arrived, first assistant Chief Ricky Holdener was on the scene. We went into the building with the stretcher and upstairs into the apartment. When I got into the bedroom, I found Theresa Smith in a Grand Mal Seizure. Michael, her husband, was in the room and I asked him if his wife had a history of seizures. He answered a resounding, "Yes."

Mr. Smith seemed agitated that we appeared to be taking so long. I explained to him his wife was stable, although unconscious. She was a heavy-set woman, and I took all the necessary precautions to assure her safety when we moved her onto the stretcher. Chief Holdener kept asking what is taking so long. I told him we needed to be certain we could move her safely. I also told him we needed a Reeves stretcher in order to get her out because she was still unconscious.

This is where the problem started. I was trying to get back into the room to work on her and Ricky Holdener was in the way. I said, "Ricky, would you please get out of the way?" He gave me a dumb look and slowly moved aside. I went into the room and started preparing to move her but I needed some help. Charlie was still at the ambulance, and when I asked Ricky Holdener to help, he turned, and walked out of the room. "Where the hell are you going?" I asked.

He looked at me with contempt and said, "I'll see you after the call." I simply ignored him and went about doing my job.

I finally got Mrs. Smith out of the bedroom and into the ambulance, and then responded to the hospital. While I was filling out the paperwork at the hospital, the unit clerk in the emergency room said I had a phone call. I picked it up and Ricky Holdener was on the other end. He told me to come to the chief's office at the completion of the call. We packed up and returned to the firehouse. When I went up to the chief's office, Ricky Holdener told me I was suspended for causing discord.

"You're out of your fucking mind, you idiot," I said. He told me to get out of the firehouse. I did. As a footnote, when a person is suspended from active duty in the Freeport Fire Department, that person is not allowed in the firehouse for any reason until the hearing. That means no calls, no matter what.

Now things got really interesting. No one had ever questioned a suspension before, and I was about to ruffle the feathers of the Freeport Fire Department like no other before.

Right away, I sent Ricky Holdener a certified, return receipt letter requesting a special meeting of the fire council to overturn this arbitrary and capricious suspension. The day he got the letter, he called me and left a message stating that I would never get a special meeting. He went on to say that he was the chief and what he said, goes. I told him, "You have two weeks to give me my hearing, in accordance with the by-laws of the Freeport Fire Department."

That was the last time I spoke to him until the night of the hearing.

During the next two weeks, I started putting together my case against Ricky Holdener. One of the things I did was to contact Michael Smith and explain to him what happened. I asked him if he would testify on my behalf at the hearing and he wholeheartedly agreed. He said, "You helped my wife, and I will do anything I can to help you."

I told him when the hearing was, and he said he would meet me there that night. I thanked him, knowing I had this thing beat. Ricky Holdener told me he had never had any medical training. Rumor had it he became chief on a bet between Don Mauersberger and another firefighter. I heard there was a discussion at Truck Company one night in 1983 where Don Mauersberger stated there wasn't anyone he couldn't get elected. John Provenzano told him he could never get Ricky Holdener elected, and Don Mauersberger took the bet.

Everyone knew Ricky Holdener lacked leadership qualities, but Don Mauersberger was out to prove a point. And prove it he did. Ricky Holdener was elected chief in 1984. To make Ricky eligible to run for the office of chief, the Freeport Fire Department changed the by-laws that a chief had to be an EMT emergency medical technician.

The hearing date was November 23, 1987 in the council room at fire headquarters. When I arrived, Ricky Holdener was already there as was Michael Smith. We made small talk and the hearing started t 9 p.m. Since Ricky Holdener was the suspending officer, he turned the meeting over to assistant Chief Julie Ellison.

Ricky presented his case. Some people in the room had a difficult time understanding him, as he appeared drunk. After he presented his case to the fire council, no one asked him any questions. I found this disturbing because everything he said was untrue. He said I pushed him out of the way. Untrue. He said I cursed him out at the scene. Untrue. He said I was disrespectful to Michael Smith. Untrue. He even said that at one point, I refused to take Theresa Smith to the hospital. That was a lie. They were all lies and no one bothered to ask any questions.

I told my side of the story. Then I asked Michael Smith, "Please tell everyone here exactly what happened." Mr. Smith stood up and told the entire fire council that I was disrespectful, rude, refused to take his wife to the hospital, that I cursed out the fire chief at the scene, and that I pushed the fire chief out of the way. He went on to say that I should not be a member of his "Beloved Freeport Fire Department."

I was speechless. I asked him if anyone had spoken to him about me since I had spoken to him in his apartment. He said, "You never came to my apartment and spoke to me."

"Mr. Smith, how much did they pay you to lie?" I asked. At that point, assistant chief Ray Maguire made a motion to go into executive session. During an executive session everyone has to leave the room so the fire council can deliberate the case in private. We all went out to the hallway to await the verdict.

While we waited, Papa Joe Flanagan went up to Michael Smith and asked him, "Why did you lie about Jon?"

"The fire chiefs said he was no good and that he had to go," he answered, contemptibly.

Joe screamed at him, turned and looked at me, and left. Right then and there, I knew something was very wrong. It had become apparent to me the railroad was coming through and that I would be on the next train out. I went up to Michael Smith and he turned and walked away from me. He walked over and talked to some guys from Truck Company and Engine Company.

I was in complete shock over what was happening and

constantly asked myself, Why would these people lie? Why would Michael Smith lie?

About fifteen minutes later, Papa Joe came back upstairs, walked up to me and said, "They had this planned for two weeks. They were going to get you no matter what you said."

I stood there in disbelief when the council room door opened and they asked me to come back in. I walked back in the room and the silence was downright frightening. Assistant chief Julie Ellison was running the hearing and he asked me to stand. I went to the middle of the room, surrounded by the fire council members.

Ellison said, "After serious discussion and deliberation, the fire council has found you guilty as charged.

It has been decided that being this is your third suspension in five years, you are hereby expelled from the Freeport Fire Department in accordance with the by-laws."

I screamed, "Are you people crazy? Show me where I was suspended three times in five years." Then I lost it altogether. I said, "I've been a member of the Freeport Fire Department for seventeen years, how can you do this?"

Ellison said, "That's the end of it. Turn in all your equipment and gear."

I looked at Ellison Maguire, Holdener, Fiore, Spinoccia, and all the others and said to each of them, "This in not the fucking end and it is far from over. I'll see you in court, you scumbags."

They sat there in stunned silence, not knowing what to say. I walked out of the council room, down the stairs, and into Rescue Company quarters.

Papa Joe was down there and was on the rampage. He was cursing, screaming at everyone and everything and throwing things. I sat at the bar and buried my head in my hands and started crying. How could I tell my father what had happened? He would be devastated and my family's name tarnished. My grandfather Pop Wright would be turning over in his grave because of what happened. The people from his firehouse, Hose 1, were involved. Julie Ellison, a guy I played Freeport Fire Department softball with for many years, was one of the ringleaders. I wondered how he would react if some of *his* skeletons were exposed.

I didn't know what to do. I had just gotten divorced from Brendan's mother Valerie, and I was staying at my father's house. Here I was, thirty-five years old, divorced, and just discarded like a piece of paper by the Freeport Fire Department after seventeen years. I didn't know who I could to turn to.

With that, my good friend Fred Jones walked into the firehouse. He had already heard what happened. He hugged me, telling me we would figure this out tomorrow. He took me to the Treehouse, got me drunk, and took me home to my dad's house.

My dad's health was failing, and that night, I lay in bed trying to figure out how I was going to tell him his son had been expelled from the Freeport Fire Department. I remember tossing and turning all night.

In the morning, Dad was already downstairs having his coffee when I came downstairs. He looked at me. "I already know."

I was speechless, embarrassed, and started crying again. I was a grown man who had been reduced to crying on my father's shoulder. He put his arm around me and said, "Are you going to let them get away with it?"

I said nothing.

"If you're not going to let them get away with it, then you better get an attorney," he said.

"I just went through a divorce Dad," I said. "I have no money for anything, let alone fighting the system."

"This is a lot more than just fighting the system. You need to make a statement." Then he added, "Don't say anything. Let this sit for a few days and start doing your homework."

Emotionally, I felt as though I had been in a train wreck and had nothing left. I agreed with him, got dressed and went to work.

I was depressed for a couple of days thinking about it. Fred called me and asked me to come over and sit with him. I went to his house that night and when I got there, some of the members of Rescue Company were there. Papa Joe, Abe Brodsky, and Zev Brandel. They started talking about how badly I had been screwed and wanted to know if I was going to fight this. I told them I had spoken to my dad and that I didn't have any money to fight this legally.

"I have a friend who is an attorney and says he will help you," Fred said.

"Fred, I don't have money for this," I told him.

Abe jumped in and said, "Don't worry, we will get Rescue Company to pay for it, but you have to lay out the money."

I told them I would have to think about it and that I would let them know. In the meantime, Fred suggested I call his attorney friend, Ray Smolenski and ask how much this would cost. The next day I called Ray, and he told me to come right over. I walked into his office he shared with another attorney, sat down, and told him my predicament.

He said it would cost fifteen hundred dollars and that he would need five hundred up front. He told me he understood my situation and that he would be flexible, but he needed the deposit to get started. I told him I would have to think long and hard about this and that if I decided to go ahead, I would contact him. I also told him it might be a couple of months before I could put the money together

That's when he told me I had a six-month window to serve the papers on the fire department. From there, he said it could take a year or longer, but the window was only six months. I told him I understood and that I had much to think about.

Days turned into weeks and weeks turned into months before I made a decision. One of the defining moments of my life came on April 10, 1988. I was holding my son Brendan in my arms at the Rec Center pool when a couple of firefighters from Engine Company walked by me, looked at me, and said, "How does it feel, being a civilian?"

If looks could kill . . . I packed up Brendan, went home, and called Ray Smolenski. I told him I was ready to kick their asses. "Ray, do whatever has to be done."

I went to his office the next afternoon and gave him money to get started and signed papers. Then I went to see my dad and told him. He looked at me and smiled. That was all I needed.

For the next few months I was nervous. I realized if I lost the case, that was the end of my fire department career, and I couldn't live with that.

I went on with my life.

In August 1988, I met the most wonderful girl in the world at the Rec Center swimming pool. Her name was Dorothy, and one day we struck up a conversation that centered on Brendan, who was five at the time. We started dating, and the rest is history. We married on April 20, 1991 and have been together since.

On April 1, 1989, I got a phone call from Ray Smolenski. "Are you sitting down?" he asked.

I said yes and he proceeded to give me the good news. Judge Johnson of the Nassau County Supreme Court ruled the fire department had acted arbitrarily and capriciously when they expelled me. He set aside their action, effectively reinstating me to full duty.

Ray went on to explain that in order for this decision to be legal, the village attorney had to be served with the decision.

It was Tuesday, April 1, 1989. On Thursday, April 4,

1989, the Freeport Fire Department would hold their annual elections. I told Ray it was imperative that I vote in the department elections. I needed to make a powerful statement.

He said his process server was on vacation for two weeks and that he couldn't do it before then. I asked him if anyone can serve the papers, and he said yes. I told him I would be right over. I would serve them myself.

When I arrived at his office, he was there waiting with everything ready. He told me what to do; I took the package from him, and went to the village attorney's office to serve the papers. The village attorney at that time was Bill Glacken, who is now the mayor. I walked in, asked for him, and the secretary told me to have a seat. It was 11 a.m. He made me sit there for an hour, when suddenly his office door opened, and he walked out.

"Bill, where are you going?" I asked.

"I'm going to lunch," he said.

I said, "Bill Glacken you are hereby served." I handed him the package with the papers and asked him for his signature. He refused. I called Ray and he said it was all right to go back into the firehouse. I thanked him, and he said to call me if there was any problem.

It was lunchtime and I was hungry, so I went to the deli and got a sandwich. I went directly to the firehouse and parked my blue van across the street. When I got out of the van, I looked across to the ramp of the firehouse, and there was Ricky Holdener standing next to his Chief's car. I walked across the street, onto the ramp, and into the firehouse. Suddenly, I hear a shout from where he was standing. I walked over to him and he said, "Where do you think you're going?"

"Inside to eat lunch."

"You're not going into my firehouse," he hollered. "You're not a member anymore."

I had three copies of the judge's order with me in case

something like this happened. I looked at him dead in the eye and said, "WRONG!"

"Get out of my firehouse," he commanded

"Ricky, you lost," I said.

"Get out or I'll have the police remove you," he threatened.

"I'll be inside eating my lunch," I said as I walked inside, sat down and started eating.

Just then I heard on the fire radio, "Police Headquarters, 2100, send a car over to fire headquarters, we have a person refusing to leave the firehouse."

I just sat there with my copies of the court order. About ten minutes later, two police officers walked in and asked me to leave. They stated the fire chief ordered me to leave because I wasn't a member anymore. Without missing a bite, I handed them a copy of the court order and looked at Ricky, who was standing behind the police officers. I said, "The judge says I can stay."

The police officers each read the court order then called for a sergeant. The sergeant read the paper, handed it back to me and said, "Enjoy your lunch," and walked out.

Ricky stood there, his face as red as an apple. I looked at him and said, "Want half a sandwich?"

He walked out cursing and screaming, saying how he was going to get me. I finished my lunch, left and went home to tell my dad.

When I got home, Dad was sitting on his back porch eating his lunch. "How you doing?" he asked.

"I won the case."

"I knew you would," he said with a grin ear to ear.

Then he asked, "Are we going to the department elections together on Thursday?"

I gave him a resounding, "Yes."

I went back to work for the day and decided to think about my strategy for the election on Thursday night.

I spoke with my dad and we agreed that since we were going to the elections together, he would drive. I called the people who'd supported me in the beginning. Fred, Abe, Papa Joe were all going to be there when I walked in.

Election night came and we headed to the firehouse to vote. Dad and I walked in the main front doors of the firehouse and got in line to vote. As soon as Ricky saw me, he came over and told me I couldn't vote because I wasn't registered. I held up a copy of the court order and said, "The judge said I can."

Everyone who was in line around us laughed out loud. Ricky was quite embarrassed. "There is no way you're going to vote in this election. I am the chief and I have final say," he said.

Again I said, "The judge says I can."

He stormed away.

By now dad and I were at the front of the line. The Freeport Fire Department Executive secretary, Allen Grosser, came up to me and said, "The chief said you have to get out of the line."

"Tell that coward to come here and tell me himself," I told him. Allan Grosser walked away, and the clerk refused to let me vote. I looked back and saw the four main conspirators in the entryway to the firehouse. They were Ricky Holdener, Ray Maguire, Julie Ellison, and Bob Terry.

I walked up and asked, "Can I talk to you four in private?"

They agreed, and we went into the old dispatcher office. Bob Terry said, "What do you want?"

I said, listen; you guys tried to get rid of me and failed because what you did was illegal. If you want to continue with this nonsense, then go ahead. I will let my attorney deal with it, and I will tell you this. If you prevent me from voting here tonight, my attorney is going to Supreme Court tomorrow morning, and each of you will end up being cited for contempt of court. You four need to remember two very important things. One, I won in court, and two, I'm not going away quietly. If you want to continue with this nonsense, go ahead. I'm going back out to the line and the only way I'm not voting is if you have me arrested."

I turned, walked out of the room, and got back in line with my dad. They continued to huddle for about ten minutes when Allan Grosser went in the room with them, emerged, came up to me with a voter registration card and asked me to sign it so I could vote. I signed it, walked into the booth, closed the curtain and voted my conscience. This was one of the defining moments of my life. I felt more than vindicated.

At the next meeting of the fire council, a new committee was formed to revamp the department by-laws . . .

~~

Finally the FDNY firefighters separated to allow me thought to the man with the injured ankle. I examined it and told him I thought it was broken. His ankle had swollen to twice its normal size and turned black and blue. We helped him down off the pile, along with other FDNY firefighters, to the waiting ambulance. When we got to the ambulance, the battalion chief who saw him on the pile thanked us for helping his man. He then told the firefighter to call his office tomorrow to report the injury. Then the chief verbally reprimanded the firefighters who wouldn't let us near his man at first.

Lt. Tucker, Charlie and I went back to the heavy rescue truck to see Captain Bentley for our next assignment. When we got there, he said, "Take five."

We all went inside the heavy rescue truck and just sat there. I think we all realized at the same time how dangerous a place we were in. Within ten minutes, we were called out again to assist another firefighter with a separated shoulder and, once again, up the pile we went.

# Fire service and friendship

Jonathan Wright and Vinnie Segreto for
Mayor Authur Thompson's funeral 1995.

Eight

# Mayor Arthur Thompson

BEFORE we got to Ground Zero, we caravanned from the Long Island Expressway, through the Midtown tunnel, and down Second Avenue. We made the left onto Second Avenue traveling south. An emergency lane had been cordoned off to allow emergency vehicles easier access to the extreme downtown Manhattan area, and there was a constant flow of them. The sight was heartening and ominous: rescue vehicles, coming to assist.

Captain Bentley commented that he thought they should have shut down Second Avenue completely to allow emergency vehicles total access to downtown without having to plot a route through traffic.

Downtown Manhattan was a disaster area traffic-wise due to the attack. Anyone going into or out of Manhattan was subject to search. Proof of this came about when we were entering the Midtown tunnel and the National Guard indiscriminately searched the fire truck in front of us. It might have been the situation, or just an over-zealous guardsman. Whatever the reason, it was a shock.

Whenever we slowed down or stopped along 2nd Avenue, bystanders cheered us on and many walked up to the fire trucks and shook the hands of the firefighters. It was invigorating, and made my adrenaline flow. I was ready for anything, or so I thought.

When we approached 23rd Street, I saw an ambulance

traveling on 2nd Avenue in the wrong direction. I thought to myself, this guy is gonna get someone killed, and I can only imagine what Captain Bentley thought. He looked at me and just smiled. When he smiled at me, I flashed back to July 19, 1995 . . .

~~

It was a hot summer day, and I was installing skylights on a house on Polk Street in Freeport. I was working alone that day because my helper called in sick. I had just finished installing the first skylight when an ambulance call was dispatched for an auto accident with multiple injuries at the intersection of Atlantic and Bayview Avenues. Daytime has always been difficult for personnel to respond because most people are working. I've made it my practice when I work in Freeport and a call is dispatched, I try to respond whether it's a fire call or an ambulance call.

I felt I had a responsibility to my community because I am self-employed and have the luxury to go to calls when others cannot. I thought if it was my family member there, I would want someone to respond, and that's why I always do it. This day was no different, so when the call was dispatched, off I went.

I responded to the firehouse to get the ambulance and found Frank Tucker waiting for me. I didn't expect him to be there because my regular driver, Joey D. always met me, sitting in the drivers' seat. When I got into the officer's seat, Joey D. would always turn to me and say, "Your chariot awaits," and to the call we would go. For some reason Joey D. wasn't there this day, and Frank was in the driver's seat. We responded to the call, and when we got there, the female driver had hit a utility pole and was unconscious.

I quickly examined her and realized she was critical. Frank and I extricated her from the car within two minutes, put her in the ambulance, and raced to the hospital. On the way to the hospital, she stopped breathing, and I had to place a tube in her throat to assist her breathing. She still had a pulse, but was in bad shape from obvious head injuries. We arrived at the hospital and turned her over to the emergency room at South Nassau Communities Hospital. The woman was hospitalized for three weeks in critical condition, but survived.

Frank and I cleaned the back of the ambulance, left the hospital, and headed back to Freeport. While driving, another call was sounded for an apartment house fire on Smith Street. We responded from the hospital, and when we got to the village line, we heard frantic calls for an ambulance to respond to Guy Lombardo and Century Court for an auto accident. The fire started from a pot on a stove that filled one floor of the apartment building with smoke. I got on the radio and called Fire Com to tell them we were responding to the auto accident.

Frank looked at me and smiled, signifying duty was calling and we would answer. Three blocks away from the call, we heard the police screaming for the ambulance to respond forthwith. Forthwith means the situation is very bad. Frank, who is always a very cautious driver, stepped on the accelerator and responded to the call with certainty. When we arrived, the police and some of the firefighters were yelling for us to hurry up and park the ambulance.

When I got out, Freeport Police officer Tom Drew ran up to me and said, "Jon, get over there fast, it's the Mayor."

I just looked at him.

He grabbed my arm and pushed me in the direction of the clearly unmarked car that was sitting on an angle to the curb and had evidently crashed into a series of parked cars.

When I approached the car, there was no one there helping the driver who was just sitting there. The driver's door was already open so I leaned over, looked in, and began my size-up. This was indeed the Mayor of our village, Arthur Thompson. Sitting in the driver's seat was the Mayor's right hand man, Andrew Hardwick. Andy and I had been friends for twenty years, and to see him with the mayor was normal. What was abnormal was seeing the Mayor unconscious and unresponsive.

I asked Andy, "What happened?"

He told me they were responding to the fire call on Smith Street. I realized this may be more serious than I thought. Andy looked like he was in a state of shock. I looked at Andy dead in the eye and said, "Andy, I need to know exactly what happened, and I need to know now."

He told me they were driving south on Guy Lombardo and Mayor Thompson looked at Andy and said, "I don't feel so good."

Andy said the Mayor immediately closed his eyes, slumped over the wheel and went unconscious. Andy started to get agitated while telling me this. While listening, I checked Mayor Thompson's vital signs. Vital signs are pulse, respirations and blood pressure, and the Mayor had NONE.

"Don't move," I said to Andy, "Just sit there." I stood back up from inside the driver's side door and yelled to my team, "This is a code, a full cardiac arrest. Get me the stretcher and the intubation kit." The intubation kit allows the medic to place a breathing tube down the patient's throat.

I saw that Frank was already on the way with the stretcher. I walked about ten feet to meet him and told him again to get the intubation kit. I took the stretcher over to the car, positioned it, and told the closest firefighter, who was John Maguire from Truck Company, to hold the stretcher. I had already checked the Mayor for any signs of trauma and there were none.

Mayor Thompson stood about six feet one inch tall. With every ounce of my strength, I grabbed him, picked him up by myself, and placed him on the stretcher. By now others had arrived to help, but I was in overdrive. Frank had prepared the intubation kit for me, so before we went any further, I attempted to intubate the patient. I carefully inserted the laryngoscope, looked down his throat, and saw what appeared to be something white blocking his airway.

"Frank, give me the Magill forceps," I said.

"Is there something in there?" he asked.

"I'm not sure," I said, "but I can't place the tube until I'm sure," I answered.

He handed me the forceps and I attempted to remove the obstruction. I couldn't grab it and so I tried to intubate him again, and this time I was successful. We placed the Mayor in the back of the ambulance and started working at a feverish pace. Frank was doing chest compressions and Tom Drew was ventilating.

We needed a driver, and the first person I saw was John Maguire from Truck Company. He is a tall man and was easy to spot. I yelled to him, "Get in the driver's seat and do exactly what I say."

He jumped in. "Okay, I'm ready."

I knew when the time came, we would be defibrillating the mayor, and I told John Maguire to be ready to stop the ambulance when I told him. I told him don't bother pulling over, just stop in the middle of the road. I told him to coordinate with the police escort we would have and tell them we would be stopping several times. While I was telling him this, Frank and Tom continued with their assigned tasks while I started the IV on the Mayor and hooked him up to the electrocardiograph (EKG).

After I hooked him up to the EKG, I quickly realized he needed to be shocked. I yelled to John Maguire, "Stop." He did exactly that, right in the middle of Merrick Road, a four-lane highway. The stop was rough and I yelled up to him, "a little smoother next time, please."

He yelled back, "No problem." I shocked my patient, but had no success. We continued to the hospital and I began administering all the advanced life support drugs the Nassau

County Protocol called for. I shocked the Mayor no less than eight times on the way to the hospital, and used every intervention I could think of, all without success. The trip to the hospital went well considering the seriousness of the situation and the patient himself. We worked like a well-oiled machine from the time we responded to the final disposition.

Upon our arrival at the hospital, we still had our escort intact. Our entourage pulling into the hospital must have been a sight to consider. After John pulled the ambulance into the bay, the back doors opened and the infantry had arrived.

"Everyone take a deep breath and let's do this calmly," I instructed. We pulled the mayor out of the ambulance and started wheeling him inside the hospital. I took over chest compressions from Frank, who had been doing them nonstop from the scene, so I knew he had to be exhausted. I stood on the edge of the stretcher while the cops and firefighters wheeled us in. We got inside and placed the mayor on the hospital stretcher and I continued chest compressions.

That's when it hit me. This was Mayor Thompson. My adrenaline kicked in and I was performing chest compressions with a vengeance. I became a machine pumping away. Dr. Mike Franklin, head of the emergency room, was the physician in charge of the Mayor and asked me for the details.

I didn't hear him at first because I was concentrating on doing perfect chest compressions. Then he yelled it out and I gave him the complete rundown without missing a compression. After five minutes, Mike Franklin put his hand on my shoulder and said, "There's not much I can do, look at him."

I screamed, "This is the Mayor of the Village of Freeport, keep fucking working." Mike apparently didn't realize who the patient was and ordered everyone to keep working. He gave high doses of cardiac drugs, one hundred percent oxygen, and just kept working at it. We worked on the mayor for forty-five minutes when he again put his hand on my shoulders and said, "Jon, it's over."

I stopped compressions, stood there with my clothes drenched in my own sweat, and broke down crying. I was inconsolable. I had just lost the mayor while he was under my care. I was helped outside by two of the nurses at the hospital, Chrissie Woerham and Joanna Presti. I was shaking and lightheaded. Chrissie put her arms around me and just held on.

I've known Chrissie for over twenty-five years, and she knew me well enough to know how bad this was. I had completely lost control of myself. Ray Maguire, John's older brother, came and tried to console me also. After about fifteen minutes, I composed myself and went back inside the hospital. When I walked in, I saw every local politician I knew standing there with tears in there eyes, except for the Freeport Republican leader, Angie Cullen. I didn't notice her crying.

I made my way back into the emergency room and knew I had to start my paper work. I also knew it had to be the most detailed report I had ever written. I went to the nearest sink and washed my face. I just stood there with my head down and then realized I hadn't seen Andy at the hospital yet. I walked out of the emergency room wondering where he was. I had to see him and went to the family room where everyone had congregated. I fought my way through the crowd and finally saw Andy standing alone in the corner of the room. I walked up to him and the only thing I could say was, "I'm sorry."

He looked at me and said, "We lost the Mayor." We looked at each other, our eyes swelled with tears, and we embraced. I soon realized that I have never felt so bad about losing someone before. But this was different. This was the

Mayor. This was the only Mayor I had ever known who actively participated in the fire department and took an active role in lending support to the troops, before, during and after calls. He was truly an anomaly.

By now the entire Village of Freeport Board of Trustees had arrived and were all consoling one another. I realized I had to complete the paperwork and made my way back to the emergency room. I also needed to call my wife. She has always been my rock. I called her and she knew right away something was terribly wrong. I told her, and she said she would be there in ten minutes. I told her not to come to the hospital, but just go home as soon as time allowed and that I would meet her there.

I sat down at the desk, grabbed a pen, and started writing. The first thing I had to write was the patient's name. Arthur Thompson. As I wrote, my hands started shaking and I had to stop, go to the sink once again and rinsed my face off. I returned to the desk and started writing again, and again started shaking. My eyes welled up and I soon realized this was the most difficult report I would ever have to write.

I kept on writing and I kept on crying. I can normally write a report in no more than ten minutes. I was forty-five minutes into writing and still, I was not done. I must have gone to the sink ten times. At one point, while describing what had happened enroute to the hospital, I went to the bathroom and vomited. Frank had offered to help, but the report was my responsibility. I was determined to finish it and did exactly that.

Just as I finished, Les Fieldsa, the senior medic in the department and former chief, showed up and I asked him to look over my report. He did and said it was fine. I went back outside to see what else had to be done, but Frank had straightened out the ambulance and was ready to go. I told him I was staying at the hospital and he agreed to take the ambulance back and put it into service. I went inside and talked to many of my friends who had arrived. The Freeport Chief of Police, Ed Locke came up to me and said," Nice job."

I looked at him and said, "Are you nuts, the Mayor is dead and you tell me nice job."

I walked away with my fists clenched, breathing hard, and ready to punch him out. I realized later on that he was only trying to help, but he went about it the wrong way, and this was the chief of police. And of course, had I hit him, I would have ended up in jail.

The next thing I saw ripped my heart out. Lin Thompson, the Mayor's wife had arrived along with their son, Greg. Greg was the spitting image of his dad, and when I realized it; my emotions got the best of me again. Lin and Greg Thompson wanted to see the body, and they were escorted into the room by the emergency room staff and some of the Village board. Lin remained composed, but Greg lost control, screaming for his father saying, "No, no, no."

I started crying again and had to leave the room. There was nothing else I could do, so I walked back to the firehouse from the hospital, about five miles. When I got there, everyone was gone. I got into my truck and went back to the job. When I got there, I cleaned up everything, told the customer what had happened, and left for home.

When I got home, Dorothy was already there and met me at the door. I looked at her and started crying all over again. She did what she was supposed to do under these circumstances. She simply held me tight. That alone made me feel better.

I was emotionally spent over this, and half an hour after I got home, I lay down and fell asleep. I was awakened by the telephone. It was Ray Maguire, and he told me the chiefs wanted me at the firehouse tonight for a critical stress debriefing. I asked him what this was, and he said it was mandatory for all the people involved on the call to attend. I told him I would be there, hung up the phone, and cried all over again. My conscience was getting the best of me.

I must have gone through the call in my mind one hundred times before the meeting at the firehouse. But still I felt agony. I kept thinking to myself, What else could I have done? Did I follow all the correct protocols? Was there really an obstruction in the Mayor's throat? Did I take too long during the intubation? Did I push the right drugs and in the right order? Did I wait too long to start the IV?

I asked myself these questions thousands of times in the next few months, and the answer is always the same. I did everything I could have; yet, the mayor was still dead. I was dreading the critical stress debriefing, probably because I had never been to one before and didn't know what to expect. I had heard rumors about what happens at these things, and I wasn't prepared to open my heart to complete strangers. I honestly didn't expect more than eight or ten people to be there, and when I walked in fifteen minutes late, there were more than fifty people there and the meeting had just started.

The first person to speak was Tom DiMaria, from the South Nassau Communities Hospital Mental Health Center. He started by telling everyone what he did and why he was there. He went on to explain that the best way for all of us to deal with this tremendous loss was to talk about it among ourselves and this was the best place to start. I soon realized why he said this.

It became abundantly clear over my many years in the fire service that firefighters hold themselves to a much higher standard, and getting them to open their hearts and talk about something of this magnitude was going to be a difficult task at best. More people came in, and the room was still silent. Tom reiterated that we needed to talk about it.

That being said, one by one, everyone in the room slowly started to open up. Ray Maguire started talking about how miserable he felt, and was followed by his brother John.

Police officer Tom Drew let his feeling be known, and then he told everyone what a great job I had done. I was uncomfortable when he spoke of me. Frank Tucker talked, and told me he thought I did an outstanding job. Ray and John Maguire echoed those thoughts. The Freeport Police Chief Ed Locke was there and cried when he started talking about it. He said, "Jon Wright's professionalism was just incredible."

I sank lower and lower into my chair because if I had done such a great job, then why was Mayor Thompson dead?

The night ended with everyone saying something and almost everyone teary-eyed, myself included. One by one we left the debriefing, and I went downstairs to my company quarters. I just sat there. I felt like the weight of the world was on my shoulders and I could do nothing right anymore. I had the Mayor under my care, he died, and I thought everyone was pointing the finger at me, as though I had done something wrong. I wanted to crawl into a hole and die.

During the next few weeks I felt myself sinking into a deep depression, but I couldn't tell anyone about it. When I went to calls, people looked and treated me differently. To this day, I can't put my finger on it, but it was still devastating. My depression climaxed when I was watching a television special about baby Jessica, who was trapped for four days in a drainage pipe in Texas. The story was about the paramedic who was in the hole with her and subsequently rescued her. The paramedic committed suicide, and I was beginning to think that was the only way out for me. I was afraid I was going to kill another person at a call and then what would everyone think.

I hit rock bottom and didn't know what to do about it. The only thing I could think about was my children and what would happen to them if I did take my own life. I knew my wife would survive, but my kids inundated my thoughts and touched my soul. It got so bad that I had it all figured out. It would be an accident on the ambulance with the defibrillator. I was going to shock myself and make it look accidental.

No one would know, and my family would be taken care of financially. My business suffered because I was unable to work at times because of the depression, and my wife was carrying the load. We were in debt up to our necks, and I was sinking fast. I was at the end of my rope.

I went to the beach one night in late October 1995 and saw the most beautiful sunset I had seen in a long time. I watched as a father walked with his two daughters on the beach, play-running away from them, and thought how great that man has things, knowing his daughters only wanted him to hold them. I saw an elderly couple walking hand in hand along the boardwalk, stop, turn to each other, and kiss. I saw a couple about my age walking together, seemingly not having a care in the world, knowing I would never be that happy again. I just wanted the pain to stop, and was ready to make it happen.

I don't know if God intervened as I sat there, but the next morning I made a couple of phone calls and started with professional counseling. I was starting to heal.

In January 1996, I heard from a friend of mine in the medical examiners office that Mayor Thompson died as a result of a ruptured aortic aneurysm. That explained many things, especially why we couldn't revive him. As time went on, I felt better with each passing day, and after several months, I started going to calls again.

Since that unforgettable day in 1995, I have had many times when I felt like the world was caving in on me, but I think of that night at the beach and I feel better.

I've also learned how to recognize the symptoms of Post Traumatic Stress Disorder, because I was diagnosed with it in early 1996. It has been a battle ever since, but I never quit, especially on myself. No dedicated firefighter ever quits.

Nine

# Kevin J. Vollmer

CAPTAIN Bentley and I were standing at the front of the heavy rescue truck each drinking a bottle of water and making small talk. Dave was a navy veteran and had some experience with mass genocide. He served during the Viet Nam conflict and had seen more than his share of catastrophe. With tears in my eyes, I told him I didn't think we were going to find anyone alive in this war zone. Six of my friends were buried in there somewhere and reality was starting to envelop me, but I wasn't going to stop at any cost.

We talked about our families, our parents, and our children. I remember saying to him that I didn't know how I was going to explain what I saw to my family. That's when I began taking lots of pictures. I took them one at a time because I didn't want to upset any of my brother firefighters. I did not want to be insensitive. Most of the pictures I took were inconspicuously taken. I took one picture of a small group of firefighters who were descending the pile. One of them looked like a firefighter from Freeport and instantly I thought back to May 1973 when I was doing maintenance to equipment on my first fire truck, Vigilant Hose Company #2 and Kevin Vollmer . . .

~~

The Memorial Day Inspection and parade was approaching. I was in the driver's compartment on the truck going through all the nozzles and adapters and all their uses. I came across the special nozzle called a Bresnin Distributor – a nozzle that had nine holes in it and was used primarily for basement fires. If the fire was too hot, a hole was cut in the floor above the fire, and the Bresnin Distributor, which was attached to a hose line, was dropped down the hole and the line was charged with water. As the water came out of the nozzle, the tip spinned as water was distributed in nine different directions, effectively extinguishing the fire. The problem with using this nozzle was it kept firefighters out of the fire building when it was in use. Because firefighters are taught the best method of firefighting is to extinguish from within; this nozzle was rarely used. That explained why it was rusty.

While I was working on this compartment, Kevin Vollmer, who was the captain at the time, and my neighbor on Park Avenue, walked up and started shooting questions at me – everything from what each adapter was to what I would do in certain situations.

"What would you do if the room you were in suddenly and without explanation, started to rumble?" he asked, and the question jolted me back to my probationary fire training.

Part of that training was to attend fire school in Oceanside, NY. The Oceanside Fire Department had their own training center and had an agreement with the Freeport Fire Department wherein we would use their facility in return for allowing some of their members to attend our fire school.

It was a Thursday night and the air was hot, heavy, and humid. Oceanside had a three-story structure that allowed them to burn on certain nights, depending on the wind direction. The building was next to a garbage dump, and if the wind was heading north, residents would not only have to bear the smell of the dumps, they'd have to smell the burning fire school as well. Consequently we could only when the wind headed south.

We left Freeport Fire Headquarters and headed to

Oceanside for fire school. The wind was south and we knew we would have a fire this night. On Hose 2's truck were Captain Vollmer, Steve Wenk, Eddie Martin driving, Froggy Sarro instructing, my brother Randy, and myself.

We arrived at the Oceanside training center and started setting up for the evolution. It was decided that I would be the nozzle man, Randy would back me up and Steve Wenk would be the officer in charge. The fire building had three floors and the fire was on the second floor. Wooden pallets were used to simulate a fire along with diesel fuel and gasoline as a catalyst. We paced in anticipation of the impending fire evolution, and Froggy went up and started the fire along with Warren Davis from Hose 1, who had arrived by car. Froggy was known for starting hot fires in fire school, and we hoped today would be no different. When Froggy returned, he walked over to us and said, with his ever-present grin, "Just wait."

We waited ten minutes for the fire to get going, and when Froggy said, "Okay," we went up to the floor below the fire and prepared to make an attack.

Randy looked at me. "Ready?"

"Ready as I'll ever be," I answered.

With that, we began to advance the line up the stairs. When we got to the second floor, I put on my air pack and Randy opened the door to the fire room. Just as he did that, someone opened the steel shutter that simulated a window. If you have seen the movie *Backdraft*, you know what happens next. The fire had been starved of oxygen, and when Randy opened the door to the fire room and the steel shutter opened, the fire was fed with a tremendous volume of oxygen, and exploded. The steel shutters were blown right off their hinges, over the fence, and landed in the garbage dump, a distance of over one hundred feet. When the fire exploded, Randy and I dove down the stairs to safety on the first floor. It was not a pretty sight.

When we regrouped, Steve Wenk decided we would use a two-and-a-half to attack the fire instead of the usual inch-and-a-half line. Simply stated, we needed more water. We finally made the initial attack on the stubborn fire and after some time, we extinguished it.

After the evolution, we returned to the truck to pack the hose. We could hardly believe what had happened. Froggy was a fire instructor who set fires in fire school many times before. And tonight, Froggy had struck again.

"Anyone for seconds?" Captain Vollmer asked sarcastically. We all laughed, finished packing the hose, and returned to the firehouse.

When we got back, Kevin Vollmer asked me to stay so he could talk to me. We stayed by the truck and he asked if I was okay. I told him I was and he asked, "What did you learn from this?"

Jokingly, I said, "Don't let Froggy start the fires anymore?"

He laughed. "Okay, now really, what did you learn?"

"The most important thing I learned today is never ventilate a fire until after a hose line is in operation," I responded.

Captain Vollmer said, "Good, remember that, it will save your life someday." He patted me on the shoulder, said goodnight, and went home.

Kevin Vollmer, in addition to being the captain of my company, was also a neighbor. He lived on the same street and we went to many fires together. He worked for Newsday and left home at 3 a.m. everyday. Being the rookie, most times I had to go out to get lunch for everyone. I remember eating my lunch while Bill Cominos and Tony Sparaco played chess on their lunch hour. They both worked for the electric department and rarely did they ever get to finish a game of chess before they had to return to work. That chessboard would sit there sometimes for a week before a game was complete, but it was never disturbed.

Kevin, Bill Cominos, Joe Walsh, Ray Mulligan, and I were at the firehouse for lunch one day in the summer of 1976 when a fire call came in for a house fire on the dead end of Bedford Avenue. We all got on the truck and responded to the call. When we turned onto the dead-end street, flames were already thirty feet in the air out of every window on the second floor. Chief Bill Casmasina was in charge.

Casmasina was assistant chief that year. He didn't make chief until 1978. When he ran for chief and lost in 1976, my dad was his campaign manager. He always held that loss against my father, and on more than one occasion, he tried to take it out on me.

On this particular day, we arrived with a full crew, and Joe Walsh was the nozzle man with me as his backup. Joe was an outstanding firefighter whom I always respected, admired, and learned from. One of the things he taught me was never aim two nozzles at each other from opposite directions. When that happens, someone always gets burned.

When we got to the fire, Ray Mulligan hit the hydrant while Joe and I advanced the first line up the front stairs to the second floor. This first line was a two-and-a-half.

Just as I walked in the front door, my brother Randy showed up and bumped me off the first line because he was senior to me. Captain Vollmer then told me to grab an inch-and-a-half and stand by the back door with the line. I did as I was told, and when I got there, I could hear Joe and Randy advancing on the fire. The fire was already vented and was still hot. That along with the high humidity made this a difficult fire to extinguish. I listened to the radio and could hear they were having trouble getting into the primary fire room. I also heard them call for another line up the front stairway. Just then, Chief Casmasina said to me, "Take that line up the ladder and put it in the window."

I gave him a dumbfounded look and he repeated his

order. I said to him, "There is fireman in that room, if I open this line up on them, someone will get killed."

"Move that line mister, that's an order," he commanded.

"I'm not getting my brother killed because you don't know what you're doing," I responded. He walked up to me and slapped me in the shoulder and said, "I'll deal with you later."

"Count on it!" I shouted.

Captain Vollmer appeared and asked what was going on. I told him I would tell him about it later.

The second line was brought in to the second floor through the front stairway and the fire was finally put out. While we were securing our equipment, Chief Casmasina walked up to me and said, "What the hell is your problem?"

I told him I didn't have any problem, and that no matter what he said; I wasn't going to help his ego by hurting other firefighters.

Just then Joe and Randy walked up to me and asked me what happened. I told them, and they said to wait. They walked up to Casmasina and had quite an argument with him. It ended with Joe getting suspended for striking a superior officer.

For three weeks, Casmasina walked around with dark sunglasses. When we returned to the firehouse, everyone came up to me and yelled at me for disobeying a direct order and in the same breath, they all said, "Good job." Captain Vollmer was tickled pink that I was able to tell the difference between idiocy and intelligence.

That was a defining moment in my life. Kevin, Joe, Randy, Ray, and Billy were my mentors and I knew it, now everyone else did too. But there would be more defining moments . . .

~~

September 12, 2001, the day after the terrorist attacks; everyone at the firehouse was edgy. We all wanted to go to

Ground Zero and help, all we could do was wait. I decided that every day, from this point on; I would religiously respond to fire headquarters and check in at the chief's office. Assistant chief Wensley, was a fixture in the chief's office. His job, also, was to wait for word on our fallen brothers.

Each day I had my morning tea; went up to the chiefs' office, and keep the vigil. I was not alone. Firefighters from every firehouse showed up to wait for the call. Ray Maguire had been into Ground Zero late the day of the attacks, and on Thursday, September 13th, he returned with a look of complete despair etched on his face and tears in his eyes. I asked him, "How bad is it"?

He responded, "Incomprehensible and indescribable," then buried his head in his hands.

Ray Maguire and John Wensley are from the same company, and I thought it best to give them their space. I went back downstairs, and as I left the room, Chief Wensley said to me, "Make sure your rig is in order." I just looked at him and walked out of the room. When I got downstairs, I called Captain Bentley and told him what Wensley had said, and that I would start going over the truck with a fine toothed-comb. This was the first sign of what was to come.

I pulled the heavy rescue truck onto the ramp of the firehouse and went through it compartment by compartment. First I opened the Hurst Tool (Jaws of Life) compartment. I pulled everything out and checked it over. I started the onboard Hurst tool generator and pulled it out, sat it down, and operated the tool and all its attachments. As I was changing the tips on the tool I remembered other years that were equally noteworthy.

1978 was an especially busy year. In March, we responded to a house fire at the intersection of Lillian and Jay Streets. With George Mulholland driving and me as the officer in charge, we pulled up to another fire where flames were already out of the second floor window when we arrived. Engine Company's truck was out of service so two of their firefighters, Joe Santorelli and Larry Fleishman, rode with us to the call. This fire was more diabolical because it was an illegal rental and there were locks on every door in the house, making entry into each room difficult.

We pulled our truck into the front of the property just past the property line. This was a corner house, and Hose 5 pulled onto Jay Street and positioned their truck accordingly. Rich VanWycklen was the driver, with John Hirte as their officer in charge and Brian Horton as the third man. We advanced on the fire with relative ease. Joe Santorelli, Brian Horton, and I made it to the second floor and opened the hose line and were in the process of making progress on the fire.

All of a sudden, the door directly in front of us flew open and flames surrounded us. We held our own for as long as we could. Then we heard the infamous rumble, meaning a backdraft was imminent. Joe and I looked at each other and at the same time said, "Let's get the hell out of here."

Brian Horton had started down when we told him to. Just then, we heard backdraft explosion we feared, and Joe and I dove headfirst down the stairway. Brian was already on the landing when we landed on top of him. We didn't know what hit us. My immediate thought was if Joe had made it out in one piece. I rolled over, looked up, and there he was.

I grabbed my helmet and told Joe and Brian to get outside for some air. Joe and I started out, and when I looked back, Brian was on the ground, as still as death. When we dove down the stairs and landed on Brian, he was knocked unconscious. Joe and I dragged him outside where he woke up and was okay.

The next thing we saw made our blood boil. We walked to the truck, looked over to Hose 5, and saw they had opened their deck gun into the window where the backdraft originated. I went ballistic and had to be restrained. Whoever ordered the deck gun in the window almost got three firefighters killed and I was going to get to the bottom of it. I fought my way loose and got over to the pump panel of Hose 5. The pump operator was nowhere to be found. I was going to tear him apart. Kevin Vollmer walked over to me, grabbed my coat, and dragged me behind one of the chief's cars. I was screaming all the way and when we got to the back of the car, he took me by the lapels, picked me up off the ground, and got into my face. He was very clear he was not going to tolerate my behavior. He was also very clear he was not going to allow whoever ordered the deck gun into the window to walk away unscathed.

I calmed down and went back to Hose 2 and washed my face off. When I did that, my neck hurt. I looked in the mirror of the truck, and saw I was burned on the left side of my neck and my hair was singed. I was pissed off.

Later that week, the chief's office investigated the incident and came to the conclusion the person who opened the deck gun in the window had misinterpreted his orders. It seems was told to set up the deck gun and not open it until everyone was out. A mistake like this can be costly in terms of firefighters getting killed. The matter was resolved, the firefighter disciplined, and the matter was put to a close. Captain Vollmer handled it well.

In July 1978, we responded to a fire at Sunrise Highway and Guy Lombardo. The alarm was transmitted and as we made the right turn in front of the firehouse, we could see flames over the railroad tracks. We pulled up and saw flames coming from three windows and smoke coming from everywhere else. This later became known as the "Tropicana fire."

The Tropicana was famous for the restaurant on the first floor and the illegal apartments on the second floor. When we pulled first in, we hit the hydrant on the corner and positioned the truck on Guy Lombardo Avenue. Truck Company pulled up on Sunrise Highway and put their aerial ladder into operation. I was a lieutenant and the officer in charge. My first responsibility was to assure everyone was safely out of the building. I went into the building with Kevin Vollmer, now an ex-captain, and we made the primary search while the other units were setting up. We quickly determined that everyone was out and that we could now proceed with our primary fire attack.

Engine Company's truck was out of service and they were using the spare rig, more affectionately known as the "pig rig."

They were positioned on Sunrise Highway adjacent to the aerial ladder. Our initial attack was made going up the stairs on the Guy Lombardo side. When we made the second floor, the smoke was thick and pungent and the hallways filled with locked doors. It was like a maze and we knew immediately we had our hands full. We knew we needed to be super careful because one wrong turn could be deadly. We didn't have any truckies with us, so we were responsible for opening our own doors.

Truck Company had moved onto Sunrise trying to make entry from the north side of the building. At first we thought we would meet up with them somewhere in the middle of the building, but because of the maze-like situation, this was impossible. After half an hour, I ordered my men out of the building and the chiefs decided an exterior attack was the safest way to go. I took my men and headed to the Sunrise Highway side. When I got there, we quickly realized that we were making no headway. Firefighters were standing around because the aerial ladder was now in operation. After fifteen minutes, Kevin and I decided to approach Chief VanWicklen and request another interior attack. I told him I thought we could make it through the Sunrise Highway side as long as the exposures were protected.

He agreed, and we were set. We were going to make this fire through the upper windows on the north side. Truck Company set up two ladders, and we started to make our way up to the second floor. I went up one ladder and Kevin went up the other. When we got to the top, a couple of guys from Engine Company started handing up the two-and-a-half we would use to attack the fire. When the hose was half way up, the fire lit up above us and we had to duck.

"Get that line up here now," I yelled down.

Just as I said that, Kevin reached for the hose, lost his balance, and fell two stories to the concrete below. I screamed and flew down the ladder to Kevin. When I got to him, he was conscious but had broken both his legs and his left wrist. The fire didn't matter to me anymore, and I went with Kevin to the hospital. The last time I had been to the hospital was when Jerry Cotignola died, and I remember thinking this can't be happening again.

Kevin was hospitalized for three days and sent home with three casts. When we got to his house, we both knew he was lucky to be alive. 1978 had been a tough year.

Kevin and I remained close friends during the next eight years. I remember him telling me he thought I should work as a paramedic, and urged me to apply for a job with the Nassau County Police Department to work on the police ambulance.

This was a hard job to land because of the politics involved. I decided to apply to New York City EMS. I did, and was hired in June 1985. I went through the academy and was finally stationed in the South Bronx, in the middle of a continual maelstrom. I worked there until I thought I had a chance to get the job with the police department.

I got that chance in 1987. I went through the proper channels and applied. I was in the process of being investigated for the job when I got the most horrible news. I was at my dad's house when the phone rang. It was Eddie Martin. He told me that Kevin was working delivering newspapers on Babylon Turnpike when someone tried to rob him. Kevin had been shot in the face and was killed instantly. I was sitting at the kitchen table at my dad's house and no one was home. I just sat there, buried my head in my arms, and cried. Kevin was gone and there was nothing I could do about it.

I thought of his children, Kevin Jr. and Vicki. I wondered who was going to tell them. Kevin loved his children dearly and spent every free minute with them. On many occasions, he'd brought them to the firehouse and let them simply hang around, as I had as a child.

I needed to go to the scene of the crime, and drove over in my pickup truck. When I got there, the crime scene was still in place. Police cars were everywhere and areas marked off with crime scene barrier. The Nassau County Police Department was there in force with their homicide van, and the crime scene van personnel taking countless pictures.

I walked up to the spot where Kevin's body had fallen to the ground and saw where they marked the body off with chalk. I broke into a cold sweat and my hands trembled. My eyes teared; I sank into a squatting positions and leaned against the building crying.

Because the crime scene was on the Freeport-Roosevelt border, some Freeport Police cars were at the scene. One of the Freeport Police officers who was an old friend of mine came up and tried to comfort me. Charlie Parker and I had been through many things together, but this was different. This hit home, and we all knew it. Charlie stood me up and told me to get myself together. He told me this was not the place, and that he would take me back to the firehouse. I got into his police car, and we went to the firehouse. He told me to get my car later.

I went inside and just sat in the driver's seat of the fire

truck for an hour until I calmed down. I was glad there were no calls during that hour. I decided to go to back into the firehouse and see what I could do to help with any funeral arrangements. When I got there, a small crowd had gathered and all very visibly shaken.

Eddie Martin, Tony Basile, and Tony Sparaco were all there and noticeably quiet, as was I. Kevin's brothers Craig and Gordon came in and told us the funeral was already set and that the fire department would be taking part in it.

I left and went to my dad's house to give my parents the bad news. When I got there, I told them and as expected, they were upset. The next two days were filled with myriad emotion on my part. I was crushed, disheartened, and embraced with anger. The police had not yet caught the murderer, and this did not bode well with me. I could only hope and pray the killer would be caught.

The day of the funeral was bright and sunny with temperatures in the lower seventies. I got to the firehouse and started wiping down the fire truck. One by one, people showed up, and at 9 a.m. we boarded the truck and went to Hungerford and Clark funeral home for the start of a long day.

By the time the service started, about three hundred mourners had gathered and the place was packed. The fire department service went smoothly, and we all headed for the trucks. Hose 2's truck was being utilized as the hearse. The poll bearers were set, and we brought the casket outside and loaded it on the truck. One of the great fire department traditions was for the hearse carrying the deceased to drive by the firehouse as a final tribute. When we arrived at the firehouse, Truck Company had their Snorkel and Aerial ladder set up as an arch for the hearse to drive under. I was in the officer's seat with George Mulholland driving, and when we drove under the arch, my body became one big goose bump. I held in my emotion with every ounce of my strength.

I was determined to maintain my composure. I was expected to because I was the officer in charge.

After we passed under the arch at the firehouse, we headed up North Main Street towards Greenfield Cemetery in Uniondale. When we approached the Freeport-Roosevelt border, fire trucks from all over Nassau County had assembled and formed arches all the way to the cemetery. I counted eight of them before we got to the cemetery and when we got there and saw the final arch, I lost it. I cried uncontrollably until we came to a stop just near the cemetery plot. I managed to pull myself together and sat there until we were told to disembark, then I got off the truck and we buried our brother Kevin.

Ten

# Timmy Higgins

WHEN we arrived back inside Ground Zero, we were the only fire truck in sight, and when I set the emergency brake, many FDNY firefighters came up to us and thanked us for being there.

Apparently there had been no FDNY fire trucks inside Ground Zero at all, so I think at that point anything was welcome. I'm convinced they would have preferred one of their own, but they were gracious and thankful regardless.

There I was, standing at the front of the heavy rescue truck preparing for yet another ascent up into the pile, dreading and anticipating what I'd find.

My safety belt had come loose, and I needed to re-secure it. Safety belts are used for countless fire-related activities, so it was in my best interest to wear it properly. While adjusting the belt, I looked to my left and saw the FDNY had positioned one of its aerial ladders inside Ground Zero. The operator was positioning the ladder in such a way as to pour water on the burning parts of the pile from a height of approximately one hundred feet. After he was raised the ladder to its final height and angle, a FDNY firefighter on the turntable below was preparing to climb up and aim the water cannon, which had been attached to the tip of the ladder. He started his laborious climb, trudging up the one-hundred foot ladder one step at a time, and I could see sweat pouring off his brow.

When he got to the top, he hooked in his safety belt, wiped off the sweat from his head, and signaled down to the operator to start the flow of water. Instantly, I envisioned the 1976 fire at 315 North Main Street, when I saw Timmy Higgins jump from a hole in the roof to the end of the aerial ladder . . .

~~

We were at the firehouse readying ourselves to go to the pub on Grove Street for a night of girls and beer. Guvnor's Pub was owned by Donnie Walis, an ex-captain of Hose 2 and a FDNY firefighter. Traditionally, Friday night was the most important night of the week for anyone who was twenty-one and single, and the pub was the place to be. Girls, girls, girls was the call of the day.

We had been at the firehouse for a couple of hours just hanging around waiting for a fire call to come in. After all, we were God's gift to firefighting. Who could best us? Not some fire, for sure. It was 9 p.m. and Timmy was his usual self, singing up a storm. Timmy liked oldies, and it was common for him to belt out a tune for no apparent reason. Tonight was the same as any other Friday night. We were waiting around for some of the others to arrive and then traipse off to the pub. Jim "Tex" Fabrizio, Robbie O'Conner, and Joey Giordano, were Friday night regulars, and we always had a good time.

It had been unusually quiet fire-wise for a couple of weeks, so we were primed for a good fire. Anxious even.

"Let's go, we're not getting any younger." Rob yelled. Nine o'clock arrived and we headed the door. Just as we did, a box call came in for North Main Street and Claurome Place.

Froggy had just walked in the firehouse and he jumped in the driver's seat. I was the officer in charge with Timmy, Jim, and Joey on the truck. Froggy pulled the truck on the ramp, made a right turn and then another right onto North Main Street. When we got to North Main and Seaman, we could clearly see smoke and flames coming from this huge house on North Main Street.

I got on the radio and broadcast, "212 to all incoming units, signal 10, working house fire, fully involved."

We pulled in and hit the hydrant right in front of the house. I stretched the first line to the front door, and Timmy had the nozzle with Jimmy backing him up. Joey had the hydrant well under control. We advanced the first line up the stairs. By the time we got up there, it was a complete inferno. The chief in charge was Spike Monestere and he assumed his duties in front of the building at his command post.

I decided it was too hot to advance without a second line for backup. I called for the second line and within two minutes it had arrived. The nozzle man was Larry Minei from Engine Company. He was an experienced firefighter. I trusted him to watch our backs. His backup was a rookie name Joe Santorelli, whom I'd known for many years before he joined the fire department.

I told Larry to stand by and Timmy, Jimmy, and I advanced the line. I opened the door, as truck company hadn't arrived as yet, and when I did, the fire roared in defiance and was hotter than I thought. Right away I called for the second line and then a third line to take the place of the second line. Larry advanced to my position, and I had both lines open up simultaneously. When they did, the room darkened down, the heat intensified, and I crawled on my stomach to the first window to the right. Timmy had followed me and Larry was still making headway on the fire.

Timmy was protecting me, because I didn't have an air pack on. Back then air packs were not mandatory, so many of us chose not to wear them. I needed to get some air from the window, and Timmy followed me over and asked if I was okay. I told him I was, and that we needed to move on this fire.

In retrospect, that was not a very intelligent decision.

With Timmy and Jimmy, we leap-frogged over Larry and Joe to the next room. When I opened that door, I found that Truck Company had already ventilated the windows and this room was considerably cooler than the first, but much larger. There was a hutch in the corner that was burning, and we extinguished it with relative ease. I found another window and took some air before moving on to the next room. I was beginning to feel tired form the smoke and heat, so I found another window.

When I next saw Timmy, he was at the same window. I had been getting a well-deserved rest. The problem was that the fire had extended into the third floor attic, which was now completely engulfed in flames and smoke. More firefighters arrived and made their way upstairs to our position. We knew we had to move fast on the attic before it took off.

Ex-captain Donnie Walis, who was also a FDNY firefighter, showed up and said to Timmy and me, "Follow me boys, I'm going to show you a thing or two." Timmy and I looked at each other and smiled. Donnie Walis' reputation was well known in firefighting circles, so we jumped at the chance to work with him. We knew we had our hands full but were determined to beat the fire. We followed Donnie into the attic and at the top of the stairs, where we had both lines ready; we opened up and progressed on the fire. After about fifteen minutes, the fire was knocked down and Truck Company had the roof opened up.

"Come over here, we'll do some truck work," Donnie yelled.

There were no truckies in sight so it was up to us to start pulling ceilings and throwing things out. Truck Company had thrown the aerial ladder up when we saw it within our reach.

"Follow me over here," Donnie said.

I followed. The problem was the ceiling beams from the

second floor that he wanted us to walk across were almost completely burned through.

He yelled out, "Watch this." With that, Donnie walked across the burnt beams on top of which he had strategically placed an attic ladder. He turned, looked back, and yelled, "Let's go, we got a fire to beat."

Timmy scooted across and as he did, he gave me that big grin of his. Then it was my turn. I am a lot bigger than those two, but I wasn't going let them get the best of me, and away I went. I started across, but my six-foot frame and two hundred pounds were just too much for the burnt beams. I landed in what was left of the bed. Donnie and Timmy howled with laughter. I stood up, shook myself off, positioned the attic ladder and climbed back up before anyone else came in the room. I had dodged the proverbial bullet.

Truck Company had the aerial ladder placed in a spot where it acted as a safety for the guys in the attic. I heard a banging on the roof and then a hole appeared. From the hole I could see one of Truck Company's finest. Vance "Vandalism" Spivey.

Van Spivey is a nice a guy. He is also the strongest human being I have ever met. On this fire, after he opened the roof, he grabbed the 2 x 8 foot roof rafter that was a good eighteen feet long, and yanked it out without any help from anyone. He had many feats of strength over the years and this was just one of them. His strength was legendary.

The overhaul was winding down and the guys started climbing down the stairs. Timmy and I were still in the attic, and the attic ladder had been removed. Through the hole in the roof I could see the end of the aerial ladder. I climbed up, got on the aerial ladder, and the operator moved it upward to clear the house. He stopped moving and I climbed down. When I got to the bottom, Timmy was still in the opening in the roof and was waiting for the aerial ladder to return to its original position. The operator pulled the ladder back but for some reason, he couldn't get any closer.

Timmy, with his ever-present grin, that "I'm too suave for words" grin, jumped the five feet to the tip of the ladder and climbed down. When he got to the bottom, he just grinned at me again.

Typical. Timmy was truly one of a kind. He loved to sing oldies and on many occasions, he belted out a tune for no rhyme or reason. September 6, 1977 was no different.

It was a Saturday night and we were readying the truck for the annual Labor Day parade in Hicksville. Timmy, Rob, George Mulholland, and I were on the ramp of the apparatus floor wiping down the truck. The skies were darkening with thunder and lightening loomed. It looked ominous out there. Others began arriving to board the trucks and head to Hicksville for the parade. Just as soon as we boarded the trucks and started to pull away, the thunder and lightening intensified, the sky opened up, and within ten minutes, the parade was cancelled.

The Freeport Fire Department had amassed around two hundred firefighters to go to Hicksville and win the parade competition.

Jonathan Wright in 1978 parade competition

This was the last parade of the year, and we were going to Hicksville with a vengeance. We had been intent on winning the final parade of the season and thus, the NY State point trophy.

The weather had claimed another victim. The Freeport Fire Department. The trophy was not going to be ours

Not this time.

We went into the firehouse and did what we did best in these conditions. PARTY. We decided if we couldn't win the trophy, then we would drink ourselves silly. We invited anyone who wanted to join us inside the company quarters. Jim had gone out back and fired up the barbeque grill, and I had gone to the beer distributor for the necessary accessories.

When I returned, the party was well under way and after about two hours, we were pretty much trashed. Some of the others had invited their girlfriends up to the firehouse, and some of them brought their friends.

Then all hell broke loose.

Hose 1, located on Southside Avenue, had come by the firehouse, stopped on the ramp, and wet everyone down that was there trying to keep cool on a hot summer night. One of the girls had a lovely dress on. It was ruined.

We were incensed and planned our retaliation. Timmy, Jimmy, Robbie, Joey G. and I decided we would wait for an hour, otherwise they might expect us. At 10 p.m. we took all the water can extinguishers and put them in my car to go to Hose 1, and wet them down through their windows.

We started down Henry Street towards Sunrise Highway and kept going past Merrick Road. When we got to the Recreation Center we had to stop for a light. While waiting for the light, a fire call was dispatched for a house fire at on Raynor Street.

Timmy, who was in the front seat, turned and looked at me and said, "Jon isn't that Raynor Street?"

"Do you mean over there?" I answered, pointing where

the flames were coming out of the first floor windows.

I pulled the car onto the fire block, and we all got out of the car. Because we had five water can extinguishers in the car, we decided to do the primary search before any of the trucks arrived at the scene.

Timmy took one can and Jim with him. I took one can and Robbie with me. I went in the front door and Timmy went in the back. The biggest part of the fire was in the front bedroom on our right side. The bed, two dressers, two end tables, and a rocking chair were burning in the room. We opened the water can on the fire and were able to contain it until the first truck arrived. Hose 1 was first in and they brought an inch-and-a-half hose line with a fog nozzle on it. It was getting too hot for us to stay in the fire, so we retreated when the others came in. Robbie and I walked outside and when we got there, we didn't see Timmy and Jim. We ran to the back of the house and just as we got there, Timmy was crawling out of the back door with a five year-old boy in his arms.

We helped him to his knees, and the little boy looked at us and said, "He saved me."

"He sure did," I responded. And thanked God that he did.

The little boy's mother ran up and grabbed him from Timmy and hugged and kissed her little Anthony.

Timmy had rescued this little boy from certain death. I had goose bumps from head to toe. We went out front and sat on the back of Hose 1's truck and by now, word was out about Timmy's heroic rescue.

Everyone in sight was coming up and offering congratulations and accolades, including the chiefs. Mayor White had shown up and offered his best words and at the same time, little Anthony ran up to Timmy, jumped in his arms, and hugged him. There went the goose bumps again.

It was after 11:30 p.m., and we had returned to the

firehouse with the water cans. We decided to start drinking again and with that, the beer flowed. We talked about Timmy's rescue and just how perfect it was. We let Timmy know how proud we were of him. This was the beginning of his fire department career. Timmy's dad was a Battalion chief in the FDNY, and I think Timmy always knew what direction his life would go. Along with his father in the FDNY, were his brothers Mike and Bobby, and his younger brother Matt, who is a NYPD sergeant. His brother Mike is the same age as I and we graduated from Freeport High School the same year. We were never close friends, but Mike was always respectful and always said hello to me.

The night continued on with beer and girls and at about 1 a.m. we started talking about how we got screwed out of the NY State point trophy. We had been drinking off and on for several hours now, and emotions were running high, especially after the fire.

In true form, Timmy yelled, "Let's have our own parade."

"You nuts?" Robbie said.

"I'll go if you go," I said.

Jim threw his two cents in. "Me too."

"Let's call other firehouses and ask them if they want to march with us," I said, "Let's go, grab anything you can to make noise, we need music."

About twenty of us went outside at 1 a.m. With pots and pans in hand, we went out to the street grabbing garbage cans and their lids, gas cans, anything we could use to make noise. It was a brazen moment, and we were on top of the world.

Here we are, a bunch of drunken firefighters, marching down Broadway, and making enough noise to wake the dead. We were having our parade, and we were letting everyone know it. One of the neighbors called the police and complained about the noise, but to no avail. When the police showed up, it was my old friend Charlie Parker. Police

Officer Charlie Parker told the complaining woman, "Lady, these boys are having marching practice."

Then he got back into his police car, turned on his rotating red and white lights, and escorted us down Broadway to Ocean Avenue and we marched right past the Freeport Police Station, at 1:30 a.m. Then we headed back to the firehouse and up onto the Long Island Railroad platform. We marched the entire length of the platform without incident until the Long Island Railroad police showed up and kicked us off the platform.

Timmy was also one of the bravest firefighters I've ever had the privilege of knowing. He was fearless in fires and out. In 1976, when I decided to branch out on my own in the construction business, I spoke to my dad about it, and he let me know he was unhappy about what I was doing. I was afraid to go out on my own, but was determined nonetheless. Timmy came up with a brainstorm about going into business together. After some thought, I agreed and the new business was born. Timmy had been working at a shop that rebuilt starter motors, generators, and alternators for cars and trucks. He told me he wasn't making enough money to support his Pontiac GTO and was willing to give it a try. We shook hands on it and started soliciting our own work. I put a roof rack on top of my green Impala, and away we went.

My father, who was still quite unhappy about it, decided to try us out, and he gave us some work to do. The first job we did together was a roof in North Baldwin. The two of us had to strip the old slate tiles off and re-roof the house. We started in the front section of the house and got all the old slate off. Just as we finished taking it off, a thunderstorm came through and we were in big trouble because even though the roof was water tight, we still had to get down off the slippery roof without getting killed. The roof was extremely wet, which made it very slippery.

The radio was blasting rock and roll music, with an

occasional oldie mixed in. We were at the peak of the roof and realized if we didn't get down quickly, we might get struck by lightening. I went first, holding onto the edge of the roof, and Timmy followed. We were slipping and sliding all over the place. Jut then the radio played a new Paul Simon song, "Slip Sliding Away." We roared with approval.

From that day forward, that was our theme song and whenever it rained, no matter if we were in the firehouse or on a job, when the song played, we stopped, sang it out loud, and paid homage to Paul Simon. "The nearer your destination, the more you're slip slidin' away," never fails to elicit emotions from us. Joyous ones.

Timmy Higgins and I remained friends until his death on September 11, 2001 at the Twin Towers of the World Trade Center . . .

~~

When word came that Timmy's body had been recovered, I was reduced to tears and hysteria. I hadn't seen Timmy for a couple of years, but I thought of him, his wife Karen and their three children often. I lost a friend, they lost a husband and a father. September 11 was real for so many people; this made it all too real for me

On October 27, 2001, Timmy was laid to rest. The funeral was set for the Roman Catholic Church in St. James, New York.

Frank Cositore, another friend of mine, had lost several friends in the attacks, and he told me he would go with me to the funeral. I had to work in the early morning, so I was unable to ride the fire truck out to the funeral. Frank picked me up at the firehouse, and we rode out in his car. When we got there, it was crowded. Over five thousand people came to pay their respects to Timmy and his family, mostly FDNY firefighters. The word awesome is overused, but it applies here. It was a heartening and somber moment, but one of solidarity.

Once we arrived and the body was marched into the church by the FDNY bagpipers, the FDNY firefighters invited all the volunteer firefighters to join their ranks. On this day, there was no separation of volunteer firefighters and professional firefighters. We were all simply firefighters.

As the casket was carried past me, I felt myself losing control. Timmy and I had been through a lot over the years, and even though I hadn't seen him for a while, it still hurt worse than anything imaginable. Tears flowed like water on a hot day.

Once inside the church, I sat among many other firefighters and paid close attention to what was being said, and I was about to experience another defining moment in my life.

Timmy had a child with special needs. Christopher Higgins was born at the same time as my son Brendan, within six months of each other. Brendan was healthy while Christopher was born with cerebral palsy and confined to a wheelchair. On the day of the funeral, I was reminded that many years had passed since I last saw Christopher, and I didn't know what to expect. It was truly awe-inspiring.

Surrounded by his Uncles Bobby, Matt, Joey, Mike and his Aunt Eileen, Christopher Higgins gave the most moving, sincere, and heartwarming eulogy I've ever experienced. Everyone in the church was inspired by what this magnanimous young man was able to do. He spoke of his father's love, his father's spirit, and his father's compassion. He told all of us how much his father loved him and how much he loved his father. He taught us all how to love unconditionally. And I am eternally grateful.

Christopher doesn't know me, but someday I hope to meet him one on one and tell him exactly how extraordinary he is. I don't think I need to tell him how great his father was. He knows. He comes from a terrific family.

When the service ended, I felt a sense of relief. I think

everyone in the church felt it. I had witnessed a son's inspiring love for his father, and vice versa. I saw men and women, fathers and sons, daughters and mothers, grandparents and grandchildren all come together to pay tribute to one person, Timmy Higgins. I saw grown men reduced to tears in a flash. I saw smiles and honor. I am fortunate to have been a part of that.

Timmy's funeral wasn't the only one I attended during the first few months after the attacks. Another Freeport firefighter, Dave Weiss, a member of FDNY Rescue 1, was also killed in the collapse. Dave was another FDNY firefighter who worked for me before he became a firefighter. He eventually branched off and owned a rubbish removal business and did work for me on many occasions. Dave was the ultimate joker, and many of us during his all too brief life, had been "Weissed" at one time or another.

I was "Weissed" at an overturn on South Ocean Avenue. When I arrived, there were many other fire trucks, chief's cars, police cars, and tow trucks on scene. My adrenalin was flowing like a river. I jumped off the truck and went to work as usual.

Dave, a lieutenant at the time, was standing on top of the overturned car and yelled, "Hurry up and get the guy out of the car."

I rushed over to the car, got down on all fours, and put my head inside. Then the laughter started. I had been "Weissed." The overturned car had been on a flatbed tow truck that took a right turn to fast and the car fell off upside down. And so, it overturned.

Everyone had a good laugh at my expense that day and when I look back, I am thankful that it happened.

Dave's memorial service was held at the Central Synagogue in midtown Manhattan the week after Timmy

Higgins' funeral. The Freeport Fire Department caravanned into Manhattan and positioned itself at Lexington Avenue and 51st Street. Freeport Tower Ladder 217 was positioned to make an arch for the march into the synagogue before and after the service.

After that day, I firmly believe anything is possible. I know it is.

FDNY tradition of having a firefighter marched into the place of worship was put to the test this day. Where else on the planet Earth could a Jewish guy from Freeport be marched into the Central Synagogue by the FDNY Emerald Society bagpipers and then after the service, march up Lexington Avenue in full FDNY tradition. It was one of the most astounding sights I have ever seen.

Inside the synagogue, Freeport former chief Jimmy Olin gave a heart-wrenching commemoration of the life of Dave Weiss. I've known Jimmy Olin for many years and his words were eloquent, sincere, and filled with love. Jimmy and Dave were very good friends, and it was appropriate to have Jimmy speak. Jimmy did a great job at possibly the most difficult task of his life. Dave Weiss was looking down on us that day, most probably thinking of a way to "Weiss" all of us.

Eleven

# My Children

WE had arrived at the final staging area outside the Millennium Hotel next to the catwalk that connected the hotel to the American Express Building. While we milled about, we had the opportunity to talk to many of the FDNY firefighters who had arrived to relieve their compatriots.

Also walking around were the support service people who offered everything from massages to spiritual counseling. It was the personification of human kindness.

Frank Tucker and I talked about all the diverse religious backgrounds we were seeing in the immediate area.

There were rabbi's, priest's, and pastors. Someone for everyone. God above was listening with many ears, hearing everybody.

I was going through the Hurst Tool compartment checking the couplings, tips, and fittings when a man with a Christian-looking religious collar approached us and asked if we would like a short prayer before entering Ground Zero.

We'd just had an eye-opening experience when the chief's aid wrote our social security numbers with indelible ink on our arms in case we were buried in the rubble from any subsequent collapses after we entered the pile. That scared the hell out of me and when this pastor or priest came over, I welcomed his gesture passionately. Nobody had ever needed a prayer as much as we did right then.

Frank and Charlie MacEneaney also accepted his

thoughts and prayers gratefully.

My hands trembled when he finished, and when I watched him move on to others who were about to begin their work on the pile, I saw some of those firefighters who were coming out of Ground Zero. They wore terrified looks on their faces. Reality was written plain and simple, right across their faces.

One firefighter collapsed when the pastor approached. We rushed over to comfort him. He was crying. When he finally got his wits about him, the pastor walked with him down the rubble-strewn street until he was out of sight. The pastor turned, looked to the heavens, clenched his hands together and asked God for strength.

I found that concept unthinkable at the time, only to find my own spirituality questioned later on that very day.

I spoke with a man named Chet from Engine 219 in Queens, and we discovered we both had a child named Brendan. His twenty-four-year-old son finished college at the University of Michigan. My eighteen-year-old had just started college at Oneonta State College in upstate New York.

The similarities didn't end there. We had both been divorced and then remarried and had another child. Time was getting short, and we ended our conversation with a handshake, a hug goodbye, and a convincing, "Be careful."

While I walked back to the rescue truck, Captain Bentley asked if I was ready to go in. Chief Wensley had been inside Ground Zero for about an hour by now and we were getting restless. Anxious. And afraid.

Another Freeport former chief, Mike Sotira surprised me from behind, and we started talking about different things. He had not been inside yet, so he also didn't know what to expect. He was there as a NYPD police officer, and he told me he was there to set up an evidence examination area inside the perimeter of Ground Zero.

He is also a member of Engine Company in Freeport so

he was friends with many of the FDNY firefighters who were lost in the collapse. We talked for another fifteen minutes, and then he went inside with his fellow officers.

I walked back to the truck once again. I saw a small pile of wreckage that had been thrown from the collapse on the ground in front on FDNY Engine 219. Inside the pile were several meaningless items, but one item got my curiosity up. I started going through the small pile and in it I found a small plastic doll called a GlowWorm, that looks like a worm with an infants head on it. Brendan had one as a small child . . .

~~

Brendan and I went to the firehouse on Sunday morning, as is our usual custom. He was three years old, and it was bagels for breakfast at the Deuce.

We walked in the firehouse and were seated at the bar when Abe Brodsky walked in with two dozen bagels and placed them on the bar. It was campaign season and bagels on Sunday mornings were a normal occurrence. Others started coming in and before long it was breakfast as usual.

"Dad, I got to go potty," Brendan said.

"Do you need help?" I asked laughing.

"I'm a big boy, I can do it."

"I know you are," I said.

He went in the bathroom and after a minute or so, I yelled, "Are you okay?"

He replied back, "I told you I was a big boy."

I continued talking to the guys on several concerns when all of a sudden the bathroom doors opened, Brendan walked out, and the room erupted with laughter. Brendan was wrapped in toilet paper and he looked like a mummy. We howled with approval.

Many times in Brendan's life things like this happened.

On November 27, 1989, Brendan and I were washing my pickup truck on the westernmost part of the firehouse ramp. I had transferred to the Rescue Company the previous month and so I now washed my vehicles at the other end.

A car drove up to the other end of the ramp, and Danny Rodriguez from Hose 2 yelled, "Jon, come over and look at this guy, he says he doesn't feel well."

"When I'm finished," I said, sure it was nothing urgent.

"Okay," Danny replied with no urgency in the request. I thought if the fellow was really sick, he would either drive to the hospital or simply go to the doctor. In either case, I didn't stop what I was doing. Besides, I had Brendan with me. Eventually I looked over, and the car the guy drove up in was still on the ramp in front of Hose 2.

"Jon, you really need to look at this guy," Danny again said.

I finished wiping my truck off as Danny walked over and grabbed my shoulder. "There is definitely something wrong with this guy, you better come over right away."

With Brendan in tow, I walked to the other side of the ramp where the car was, opened the car door and asked, "What's wrong?"

The guy fell out of the car, obviously unconscious. I rolled him over and discovered four stab wounds to his chest. I looked up and saw Brendan staring down at the guy.

I took him by the arm, sat him down about twenty-five away, grabbed a portable radio, and requested help from the fire department and police department.

As soon as I said that, people came out of the woodwork to help. I will always remember the look on Brendan's face when he saw the guy.

Although Brendan's mother and I were divorced, Brendan always managed to spend time at the firehouse with me, just as I did with my father.

But lately, because of the problems I had with the fire department and certain members who always took it upon themselves to cause trouble, I decided to shelter my nine year-old son, Christian. I didn't want to expose him to the nonsense Brendan had seen.

Throughout the 90s things were normal at the firehouse, with fires, ambulance calls and every kind of emergency. I saw people die, babies born, children with broken arms and elderly people with heart conditions.

I saw people burned out of house and home and I saw thirty carpenters, who had never seen each other before; build a handicap accessible extension on a house in Freeport in one day, for a girl who had been seriously injured in an auto accident.

But even after all my emergency experiences, absolutely nothing could have prepared me for the events of October 21, 2000 on the football field at Mepham High School in North Bellmore, New York.

Brendan had entered Mepham in September 1997. He was always a gifted athlete, and I knew he would have a stellar four years in high school athletically as well as scholastically. He started playing Pee Wee football at age eight and excelled back then. He was always the starting quarterback and was constantly getting pummeled. He took more than his share of hits, which, in turn, made him tough both mentally and physically.

As time went on and he grew, his arm strength was well above average, and he could throw a football abnormally, Herculean, long distances. This continued into high school and when he got there, I told him I would do whatever I needed to do to help him and his team.

His head coach, Kevin McElroy, contacted me and asked me to be the team statistician. I gladly agreed, and thus began my career on the coaching support staff of the Mepham Pirates. I was responsible for charting all the plays that occurred during the game, how many yards gained, everything that happened on the field, and I was glad to do it.

After Brendan graduated from high school, I remained on the staff and still perform my duties to this day. Brendan continued to play and draw attention. I may sound prejudiced, but the stats and videotape don't lie. Truth is, I'm a proud dad. But facts back up the pride with truth.

Brendan's four high school years were filled with the usual teenage high school idiocy, the same kind of stupidity I'd tried with my parents (I didn't get away with it either). Cutting classes, girls, food fights, and party, party, party, were part of everyday life. Brendan still doesn't believe I was his age once.

Then came October 21, 2000. During the high school football season, my days were pretty busy. I would leave my house by 7:30 a.m., get my newspapers, and go to Eisenhower Park for my daily walk. I would walk for forty-five minutes to one hour and then retire to the workout room. After my workout, it was into the whirlpool, shower, off to see my customers, and breakfast. I was usually finished with breakfast by 10:30 a.m. and then I would go to Mepham High School for pre-game warm-ups and final game planning with the coaches.

If we played at home, which was the case on October 21, the visiting team would arrive anywhere between 12:30 and 1:00 p.m. for a 2:00 p.m. game time. The Hewlett High School Bulldogs arrived at 12:30 p.m. sharp, under the direction of head coach Jay Iaquinta.

In athletic circles, coaches know each other in different capacities, and I had known Jay for about three years. We met at Central Sport Care during the rehabilitation of my left knee after surgery. He was also rehabilitating his knee. We would often talk during our rehab sessions and although we were never really good friends, I had built a rapport with him. Outside rehab, we would always say hello to each other on the football field or not.

Jay also knew my son was an exceptional football player

and often asked how Brendan was. When they arrived at the field that day, I walked up to him and said hello and he reciprocated, then it was down to business as usual. During warm-ups, I would warm up the kickers, in this case Christian and Rocco. At 1:30, the entire team would go back into the locker rooms for final preparations and speeches by the coaches.

I'd been around football for many years by this time, and I'm was amazed at how well Kevin McElroy motivated his players and got the best out of each and every one of them. He remains an incredibly talented head coach, and I have been fortunate to work with him week in and week out during football season. I have seen him work his magic daily for the past six years, and he never ceases to amaze me.

The Hewlett Bulldogs and Mepham Pirates have been Conference II rivals for many years and that day was no different. We had to at least tie them to assure a playoff spot.

Game time arrived at 2:00 p.m. and the Mepham Pirates kicked off to the Hewlett Bulldogs. On the first set of downs, Hewlett was unable to move the ball. They punted to Mepham, and Mepham moved the ball down the field and eventually had to punt. When Hewlett got the ball back, they began to move the ball ever so slowly down the field.

The week before each game, we sent out scouts. The week before this game, we sent Charlie McShea to videotape Hewlett and watch their key players. Charlie is a former Mepham football player. We watched the tape and knew what players we had to key on.

The Hewlett coaching staff does precisely the same thing. This game was testament to their preparation. During the game, I was up in the booth charting as usual, and on the eighteenth or nineteenth play of the game, a Mepham player went down. I continued charting, but also watched closely when the coaches ran on the field.

At that moment, I got a call on my headset from the

sideline. They told me to go to the field immediately. Brendan was hurt. I looked down again, and Brendan was still laying there and not moving. My heart raced, I got a knot in my stomach, and I broke into a sweat.

I started climbing down the ladder thinking about what could have happened to my son. As soon as I got to the bottom of the ladder from the booth, I ran as fast as I could.

The security guards at the gate saw me coming, opened the gate, and stepped out of the way. By now I was out of breath, but I kept running. When I got on the field I started walking from about fifty feet away. I didn't want Brendan to see me panicking. If I stayed calm, he would too.

I kept my cool and walked over, kneeled on one knee, and asked Brendan where it hurt. He turned his head and said, "My left elbow."

"What happened," I asked?

I saw that his elbow was dislocated. His upper arm and lower arm were completely separated, only held together by skin. I had seen injuries like this innumerable times before, so I knew after a trip to the hospital, he would eventually be all right.

"Brendan, you're going to be fine," I said, and I knew he would be. I put my hand on his shoulder, patted him, and by my look, he knew he would be all right.

As I started to stand up, he grabbed my arm, and said, "Dad, he did it on purpose."

"What do you mean?"

"The guy chopped my arm three or four times and broke it intentionally."

"What did you say?"

"Dad, he broke it on purpose," Brendan repeated.

I headed over to the Hewlett bench screaming a profanity-laced tirade.

"Who the fuck did this to my boy? I'll kill him." And I meant it. "Mepham, go out there and kick their motherfucking asses."

Just then Head Coach Kevin McElroy ran over to me with assistant coach Buster Woloski and grabbed me and told me to get off the field.

"I'll kill whoever did this," I threatened again.

It took four people to hold me back. My shirt was torn and my glasses broken. I was incensed about what this coward did to my son, and I wasn't going to let him get away with it. I went after the Hewlett coach Jay Iaquinta and one of his assistants. Finally, Kevin McElroy grabbed me and physically had to remove me from the field.

By the time I got to the Mepham sideline, I had calmed down a little and I was able to help Brendan over to the bench. An ambulance had been summoned, and I waited with him on the sideline.

In retrospect, it must have been incredibly difficult for Brendan to go to the hospital. He was the Captain of the football team and the leader both on and off the field. I cannot imagine what he felt emotionally. Certainly he must have felt he let his teammates down.

The ambulance arrived, and I helped Brendan into it. When he stepped into the rear door, he had a big step up.

With one motion, he lunged forward and screamed in pain. He looked pale and sweaty with pain embossed on his face. He managed to sit down on the bench, and we went to the hospital.

On the way to the hospital, the driver of the ambulance made a wrong turn and got lost. What is normally a ten minute ride took over half an hour.

The North Bellmore Fire Department did not have an Emergency Medical Technician on the ambulance, so I was medically in charge of Brendan and subsequently had to fill out the Pre-Hospital Care report. It was one of the most difficult reports I've ever had to complete. Brendan was in considerable pain all the way to the hospital, and that made me uncomfortable, but I couldn't let on to Brendan that his pain upset me. I had a knot in stomach that would not let up.

We arrived at the hospital at around 3 p.m. and they were waiting for us. I had called ahead on my cell phone and when we walked in, several of the nurses who were friends converged on us.

They immediately took Brendan to a bed and painstakingly removed his football uniform. I was resigned to the fact that he was finished with football for his senior year. Patricia Salsone was the nurse in charge of Brendan's direct care, and I asked her to cut his football jersey off in a manner where I would still be able to frame it for him.

She did a great job and the jersey is hanging in my living room, among Brendan's many pictures. Just as soon as Brendan was in a hospital gown, the emergency room doctor came over and examined him. Brendan's arm was so grotesquely deformed, the doctor called for an orthopedist.

Within five minutes the in-house orthopedist was with Brendan and me and ordered x-rays. He also gave Brendan an injection to relieve the excruciating pain.

Brendan's mother had arrived at the hospital at the same time, and she and I met with the doctor. He told us Brendan's arm was completely dislocated at the elbow and that he also had two hairline fractures. He went on to tell us that although it looked very bad, the injury itself was relatively simple to repair. He told us that Brendan would have to undergo conscious sedation. He explained that several drugs would be administered intravenously that would relax him.

Valerie and I both agreed and signed the consent form. There was no way I was going to leave my son alone in the room while they performed this procedure. Valerie went outside, and I stayed while they gave Brendan the injection.

The doctor and I talked for ten minutes until he thought Brendan was sedated almost to the point of unconsciousness. I assisted the doctor and nurse to position Brendan. He didn't know what he was in for. I leaned over and explained what was about to happen, kissed him on the forehead, and told him I loved him. When he told me he loved me too, the tears started.

The doctor held Brendan's left arm firmly while I braced his shoulders. The doctor tried to pop his elbow back in. Brendan screamed in agony, "Dad, please make them stop, they're killing me."

"It's alright, it'll be over in a minute," I said.

He kept screaming for them to stop, and I hugged him as hard as I could, and kept telling him how much I loved him. It seemed like an eternity but in reality was only about a minute and a half. Apparently the doctor underestimated how physically strong Brendan was, because he was not able to pop it back in on the first attempt. He stopped and ordered the nurse to double the dosage of the drugs she had given him. I knew they would take ten minutes to work, so I told Brendan I would be right back and went out to tell the people who had gathered, Dorothy, Valerie, Amber, who was Brendan's girlfriend, and some of Brendan's other friends, what was going on. As soon as I walked out of sight of Brendan, I broke down crying, went to my knees and prayed for this to end. Begged for it to be over and for my son to be okay.

My wife Dorothy came right over to me and held me. She told me to get myself together because otherwise everyone would be crying. I managed to calm down and explain to everybody what was happening, and then I went back into the room. While I was walking back to the room, I thought to myself, "What kind of father am I to let the doctor hurt my son like this?"

I also remembered why we were here in the first place and my anger boiled again. I went into the bathroom and composed myself, then returned to Brendan's room.

When I re-entered Brendan's room, the doctor was ready

for the second attempt. "Let's do this," I said.

I grabbed Brendan once again and the doctor took hold of Brendan's left arm. I nodded my head, and he started. Again, Brendan writhed in agony and after another two unsuccessful minutes, the doctor stopped.

"I told you he was strong," I said. Then he suggested he could completely anesthetize Brendan.

"You do whatever you think you need to do to stop my son's pain."

I went back outside to tell everyone what was going to happen next, but I couldn't find Valerie. I looked for her for five minutes. When I found her, she told me I must have passed her and that she was in with Brendan.

She told me that when I left the room, the doctor was still holding Brendan's elbow and that he tried again. As soon as the doctor let go of his elbow, it popped back in by itself. I looked to the heavens and said thanks because I don't know if I could have gone through the emotional havoc again.

I walked outside the hospital emergency room and cried for a few minutes until my wife came over to me and told me she loved me. I went back inside and helped prepare Brendan to leave the hospital. I knew it would be a couple of hours until he could leave, because the drugs had to wear off. When they did, Brendan walked out on his own.

Once Valerie, Brendan, Amber, and I were in the car, we left the hospital and headed for Mepham High School where Amber's car was parked. When we got there, Brendan was still groggy from the drugs, but he insisted on walking Amber to her car. I found that remarkable given the circumstances. He kissed her goodbye, I got into my truck, and we left together and headed for Brendan's house.

When we got there, I helped Brendan inside and put him in his bed. His mother and I talked for a while before I left for home. When I got to my truck I had a message on my cell phone to call Kevin McElroy.

I called him, and he told me to meet him at the school on Monday because he had something he wanted me to see. I agreed and told him I would see him Monday morning.

When I got home, my wife and Christian walked outside and just hugged me. It was the best feeling of the day for me. I had been through a lot that day and compassion was welcome.

Assistant coach Buster Woloski called me at 8 p.m. to tell me that Hewlett High School head coach Jay Iaquinta and his staff reviewed the football films on Sunday mornings. I knew where I was going on Sunday morning.

I woke at 6 a.m. Sunday morning and told my wife I would be back in a couple of hours. I went to get my morning papers and set off to Hewlett High School in search of Jay Iaquinta.

The custodian at the school steered me in the right direction and I walked into the locker room at 8 a.m. I had to search a little bit but soon found the coach's office with all the coaches in it.

I had a hat and dark glasses on and Jay Iaquinta saw me, walked out of his office and said, "Can I help you?"

I took off my glasses. "Yes."

"Jon, what are you doing here?"

"We need to talk in private."

"Follow me."

When we got to another part of the locker room he turned and said, "Jon, what's up?"

"Jay, we have a serious problem." He looked perplexed and asked, "What's wrong?"

I told him, "One of your football players intentionally hurt my son, and he is out for the year and maybe his college career."

"Is number fifteen your son?" He asked. There was no hesitation in his voice.

I didn't even have to answer him. His chin hit the floor when he realized who my son was and what had happened. His eyes teared and he remained speechless.

"Jay, by tomorrow afternoon, I want a meeting with you, your football staff, your athletic director, and school principle," I told him.

"I'll call you tomorrow morning."

I gave him my cell phone number and left the school, but didn't miss the concerned look on his face. I went home and spent the rest of the day with Brendan.

By 10 a.m. the next morning I hadn't heard from Jay and decided to call Hewlett high school. I spoke to the athletic director and he told me he would call me back by 3 p.m. that day. He never returned my call.

Between 10 a.m. and 3 p.m., I went to the high school and saw Kevin McElroy. Before I saw him I stopped in Mike Muscara's office. Mike was Mepham's athletic director, and he told me not to over react when I went to Kevin's classroom. He put his arm on my shoulder, said it again and walked with me upstairs.

When we got there, we walked into Kevin's classroom and he told his football team to leave the room. They were all there and had seen what I was about to see. The looks on their faces concerned me and so I sat down and Kevin turned on the videotape machine. What I saw next turned my stomach.

The Hewlett football player who assaulted Brendan was caught on videotape from three different angles. After he played it the first time, Kevin leaned over and said, "Breathe, Jon."

"Play it again," I demanded.

He played it again and this time I got mad, stood up, and threw a chair. Kevin grabbed me and said, "Jon, calm yourself down."

I looked at him and Mike and said, "Calm down, are you

fucking crazy?" Not the best example to set in a high school, I'll admit that, but anger coursed through my veins.

Mike stood in front of his door – probably because he thought I might leave and do something stupid. He is incredibly insightful. I sat there for fifteen minutes and watched the tape time and time again. When I was able to calm myself down, I said, "I'm going for a walk, I'll be back."

I walked the halls of Mepham High School for what seemed an eternity. When I returned to Kevin's classroom, I thanked him and told him I would call him later that night. I had to find Valerie and tell her what I had seen. This would not be easy because she gets highly emotional at times, more so than I.

Brendan had gone to school on that Monday and I found that to be a true show of his character. I thought I would tell her while he was in school. He had already seen the videotape and was clearly unhappy and let it be known how badly he would like to meet this guy. I also had to take him to the doctor on Monday afternoon so I knew he would be occupied with that.

When we got to the doctor's office, he was nervous and pacing aimlessly. We went into the examination room, and the doctor confirmed what I already knew in my heart. Brendan's high school football career and possibly his college football career were over. I watched as the doctor told him. His eyes filled with tears and he clenched his fists. This was not a good sign. Then he said something to the doctor that set me back.

"Doc, I want to play in the playoffs at Hofstra in three weeks."

"Forget it Brendan," I said. "I'm not going to let you jeopardize your future for a football game."

"Doc," he asked, "if I rehab every day and wear a special brace, can I play in three weeks?"

"Very, very doubtful," Doctor Lee answered.

Brendan walked out of the room and said to Jeff Corbin, the athletic trainer, "let's get started."

The rest is history.

For the next three weeks, Brendan was a fixture at Central Sports Care, the rehab center in charge of his physical therapy. I went with him as often as I could. Going into the third week, I became apprehensive about the possibility that he might actually do it.

On Monday of the third week, I called Jeff and asked if this might actually happen. He told me the possibility existed and that he wanted to know what I wanted him to do.

He told me if I didn't want Brendan to play, then Brendan would not pass his last physical. I told him I would let him know. I called Valerie and relayed what Jeff told me. She said that Brendan would be devastated if he didn't play. That was something I already knew. I called Jeff back and asked him if Brendan would be safe from further injury if he played.

"Brendan will be fine if he wears the brace I ordered for him."

"What will the brace do?" I asked.

"Lock his elbow in one position and he won't be able to move it," he said.

I turned to Jeff. "What do you really think?"

"If he does everything I tell him to do," he said, "he'll be fine, but he must wear the brace."

I told him Brendan could play.

I went with Brendan to Jeff's that Friday and was amazed when Jeff gave him the news. Brendan couldn't get out of there fast enough. I drove him directly to the practice field and we told the coaches. We didn't tell the team just so we could see how this drama would play itself out.

The practice field is about three hundred yards from the locker room, and when the first player saw Brendan running with his practice gear, he yelled to the others and they all ran to meet Brendan. My eyes teared and this was a sign of what was to come at Hofstra on November 5, 2000.

Brendan had worked incredibly hard to rehab himself. I never thought he could do it, but he proved me wrong. The final practices went as expected with Brendan right in the thick of things. Kevin McElroy decided that Brendan would only play defense because he is such a ball hawk and impact player. Brendan was also the backup quarterback and knew the offense better than anyone. When the offense was on the field, Brendan often played wide receiver and tail back.

During that week, I had received word that the player who assaulted Brendan on the football field was going to play in the playoffs. I was furious that Hewlett head coach Jay Iaquinta would entertain the notion that this kid should play.

Apparently this kid's parents threatened the school district with litigation if they kept him off the team. When I heard this, I wrote a scathing letter of protest to Pat Piscarelli, who is the head of Section VIII football, the governing body in Nassau County. I reminded him that the player who assaulted and intentionally injured my son had been immediately ejected from the game and suspended from the league.

I also told him that I have the videotape and that I was not afraid to make it public. Section VIII called a special meeting and the player was suspended from playing for the remainder of the football year. It was a shame that it came to this because all the Hewlett High School district had to do was suspend the player. Some people are just cowards.

Saturday, game day arrived, and I was nervous as a cat on a hot tin roof. When I got to Mepham High School for the preparations, I paced incessantly. Kevin McElroy told me a dozen times to stay calm and just let Brendan play. My hands were sweating, and my heart pumping a hundred miles an hour.

Kevin addressed the team, and we boarded the bus and headed for Hofstra.

When we arrived, we were given the home team locker room and made our final preparations. My duty that day was to be in the television booth and act as a spotter for the television announcers. I made my way to the top of the grandstand and entered the booth. When I got there, the two announcers were talking about Brendan and were wondering if he was indeed going to play. I decided it was best to keep my mouth shut until after the game and not tell them who I was.

That was about to become another defining moment in my life. Mepham was playing Garden City and after the playing of the national anthem, the player introductions started.

As each player was introduced, his name and picture went up on the mammoth screen, and the player ran onto the field. Brendan was the last player announced and it went like this:

"Ladies and gentleman, last but certainly no least, Team Captain and starting strong safety, Brendan Wright."

Brendan ran through the goalposts to his waiting teammates and they swarmed him. The crowd gave Brendan a five-minute standing ovation.

I was nothing but tears and goose bumps. A proud dad, to say the least. Luckily, the announcers never turned around to see me on the verge of hysteria. I was able to maintain my composure, and the game began.

Garden City was the heavy favorite but when the game started, Mepham controlled them like a kid playing with marbles. They couldn't do anything until about one minute remained in the first half, and they scored a touchdown on a broken play.

When the second half started, Garden City scored again and eventually went on to win the game. During the second half, the starting quarterback for Mepham got hurt and Brendan was forced into action as the quarterback. He played remarkably well with only one arm. When the game ended, Brendan led the game in tackles, intercepted a pass, recovered a fumble, and threw a touchdown pass. Not bad for the backup.

Also in attendance were professional photographers who took several action shots of Brendan playing. I have three of them hanging proudly in my home. All three pictures show Brendan in action with his arm in the brace and locked in position, unable to move.

Although they lost the game, Brendan led his team by example and they responded to him. No man could be prouder of his son than I was that day. November 5, 2000 had become the proudest day of my life . . .

~~

Once again I focused on my job at Ground Zero. I picked up the glow worm and put it in the heavy rescue truck. Just as I did that, Chief Wensley called me on the radio and told me to get ready to come inside. We all looked at each other, took a deep breath, and boarded the truck. Our lives were about to change.

Twelve

# Meeting Mike and going home

IT was 7 a.m. on September 15, 2001, and Chief Wensley had just received word that we had been relieved to go home after forty-eight grueling hours in hell.

Captain Bentley had gone through every cabinet on the truck and made a list of the equipment we had used and had to find. This was going to be a task because we had equipment all over Ground Zero.

Charlie Manning and I teamed up and started our final climb of the day up into the pile. We followed the electric lines we had laid when we first arrived. They led to our lights and the FDNY ladder truck with the six fatalities onboard. All the victims had been removed and we were able to remove our lights, lines and bolt cutters.

Captain Bentley and Lt. Tucker started reeling in the electric line when I realized it was almost five hundred feet long. I looked back at the truck and it looked like a Tonka toy in the distance. Although it was small, the sight of our heavy rescue truck among all the rescue workers was truly majestic. The red and white lights were going and the only thing you could see was the plethora of FDNY fire helmets and coats surrounding it with the black and yellow electric lines intertwined. My pride was in overdrive.

Slowly and methodically, Charlie and I worked our way back to the truck, inch by inch. When we got to the truck, the swarm of FDNY helmets and coats parted like the Red Sea and we finished stowing the line.

Next we had to find the three Halligan tools, two sets of bolt cutters, numerous hand lights, and other assorted tools, but the most important was the Hurst Tool (Jaws of Life). We had taken it into the pile about twelve hours before to try and free another body from its imperiled position. I was working inside a corridor formed by the fallen steel, and when we searched it, we found the body of a young man pinned under the beam with only his feet showing.

It took several hours to free and remove his body. I was particularly moved because when we finally removed him, he had a cross of Christian faith around his neck. It fell off and I picked it up and placed it in his pocket. I did so without looking at what was left of his head. It was macabre.

It took some time before we found the tool. We didn't have a line to follow because we'd used the portable generator. When we did find it, it was a considerable distance from the truck and in a precarious position. We had a lot of help from the FDNY firefighters when we started moving the Hurst Tool, as it is very heavy, and we welcomed the help. Everybody remarked about what a great tool this was and how well it worked. I took personal satisfaction because I was the Chief Driver of the heavy rescue, and the truck and everything on it were my responsibility. It was great to be appreciated.

By 8 a.m. we had everything back on the truck. Many FDNY firefighters came over and thanked us for our help. Those gestures were cherished by all. We would be forever bonded to all of these firefighters by Ground Zero.

I climbed into the driver's seat of the heavy rescue, looked over to Captain Bentley, and put the truck into reverse. I had to back it out of the pile carefully because debris was still scattered everywhere. One the FDNY chiefs guided me until I was able to straighten out. I put the truck in drive and inched forward. As I did, every firefighter, police

officer and rescue worker waved to us with a smile. Captain
Bentley and I looked at each other in amazement. I looked in
the rear view mirror and everyone was watching us. It was a
great feeling.

We were all exhausted and looked forward to getting
home to our families. Inching forward, I noticed the huge
wrecking ball that had been in our way when we first entered
Ground Zero. It was now acting as a counter weight for the
crane it was mounted on. When I went past it, I said to
Captain Bentley, "If this thing drops on us, we'll be squashed
like a bug." He smiled and said, "I need a beer." How many
times had I heard that remark . . .

~~

We were in the heat of a warm spring in 1971. My
brother Randy, at home with me and my mom, said, "Let's go
to McDonalds."

I was hungry and eagerly obliged. We jumped into his
bronze Volkswagen Beetle and drove to his best friend
Kevin's house on Center Street. When we pulled in front,
Randy beeped, and Kevin came running out and got in the
car.

"I'm starved," I said.

"Yeah, and I'm thirsty," Kevin gave me a quirky look.

McDonald's was on Merrick Road in Merrick, NY and
when we pulled away from Kevin's house, Randy made a U
turn and headed to south Freeport.

"Where are you taking me?" I asked.

"Relax, you'll see."

I was really wondering what these two were up to. I was
sixteen and had to be home by 9:30 p.m. because I had
school in the morning and lacrosse practice the same
afternoon. When we got to Atlantic Avenue, Randy made a
left turn heading towards Baldwin, NY. Now I was totally
confused until we turned into the T & L Beer Distributor on
Atlantic Avenue. It suddenly became quite clear why we were

there. BEER!

Kevin and Randy told me to wait in the car and they went inside. When they came out, they had three cases of Schaeffer Beer. One for each of us. My dreams came true thanks to my big brother. This was going to be a great night. We headed to the McDonald's in Merrick. When we got there, we all went inside and got burgers and fries. The night was shaping up to be stupendous.

We went back to the car and proceeded to eat our food and drink ourselves into oblivion. As the time passed, it became obvious to me that this was a Tuesday night tradition among Randy and Kevin's friends. Kim showed up, George arrived and some others. We had effectively taken over the small McDonald's parking lot.

It was now approaching 10:30, and I told Randy I had school in the morning and had to go home.

He yelled back, Relax, Mom and Dad know you're with me. Its okay."

I shook my head with approval and kept drinking. We were having so much fun it hurt. We were chasing girls around the parking lot when a Nassau County Police car drove up. I was scared silly and ran into the bathroom. I was pretty drunk and thought the police would take me home, and then I would be in big trouble with my parents. I stayed in the bathroom until the police left, and when I returned to the car, I told Randy he had to take me home. "Now." I was drunk as a skunk and didn't know enough to care.

It was 12:30 a.m. when we drove out of the parking lot. I knew I was in big trouble when I got home. I walked up to the front porch, turned and looked at Randy and Kevin who were watching me and laughing. They waved and said, "Good luck."

I climbed the old brick steps to the front porch of our house, put my key in the door and opened it. Standing there was my father. I stood silent for what seemed an eternity when my father asked, "Where the hell have you been?"

I knew I was caught. "I was with Randy and Kevin drinking beer at McDonald's."

I was laughing as I said it. The next thing I remembered was landing in our neighbor's driveway next to his front porch. His driveway mirrored ours. I figured out that when my dad hit me, I went flying about fifteen feet before I finally stopped. I didn't know what hit me at first but when I stood up and looked at my dad, he just closed the front door without saying a word.

I thought it best to sleep on the back porch that night, and when I woke up, my mother was in the kitchen making my dad's breakfast. Quietly, I went into the kitchen, and my mom just gave me a disappointed look. I sat at the table and she leaned toward me. "Do you know why your father was so angry?"

I looked at her dumbfounded and said, "Yeah, because I got drunk last night."

She kissed me on the head and said, "No, he was mad because you didn't call and tell us you would be late. We knew you were with Randy, but you didn't call." She continued. "I was worried sick that something had happened to you, and we didn't know what you were doing or where you were. We weren't mad that you got drunk. We always knew you would try it. We just didn't know where you were." A lesson learned . . .

~~

While a beer right now sounded good, getting home sounded even better. I inched forward, made a left turn and saw an area that had been cleared where the debris buckets were being emptied. I watched as each bucket's contents were carefully scrutinized for remains and clues. One FDNY firefighter I watched called a supervising chief over and showed him something in one of the buckets. The chief motioned for someone from the NYPD crime scene tent to come over and look into the bucket. We were stopped for a couple of minutes while a tractor trailer was positioned to remove the massive debris piles that were now forming. The NYPD officer took the bucket to the tent, and I watched as he emptied the bucket of what appeared to be a flap of skin with a pair of tweezers. Only ten feet from me, and I could clearly see what he was doing, and it sent chills down my spine when the officer held it up to the light.

I moved forward again and saw the catwalk we came under when we entered Ground Zero and the checkpoint the NYPD had set up that no one passed without being checked. They had been there when we came in, but not in such numbers. I approached the catwalk and Captain Bentley yelled, "Stop."

"Why," I asked.

"I need to check and make sure you don't hit the catwalk."

"Good thinking."

"That's why I'm the Captain," he answered.

I laughed heartily and leaned out while he checked. We had three inches clearance.

Just before I went under the catwalk, I stopped, stepped on the side board of the truck and looked back at the obliteration behind us. I sat in the driver's seat and held my head in my hands for a few seconds.

Captain Bentley simply said, "I know."

I shook my head in agreement. I pulled forward and went under the catwalk. Straight ahead of me was the waterfront and I could see Air Force jet fighters looming in the distance. It made me uncomfortable.

As I made the left turn onto Liberty Street, all the support workers waved to us and many of them yelled out, "Good job Freeport." That was music to my ears.

I looked in the rear view mirror and saw the carnage once again with plumes of thick smoke billowing upwards towards the heavens. This time I cried inside, and it made me feel like I would explode. I drove slowly forward as the road was now more crowded than when we went in. FDNY fire trucks lined the streets wherever we looked, and still connected to the hydrant outside the Millennium Hotel was FDNY Engine Company 219. The same firefighter was still pumping the truck to the tower ladder inside Ground Zero. He looked up, waved, and mouthed, "Thank you," to me. I saluted him in return, as did Captain Bentley.

I told Captain Bentley I thought this was going to take a very long time to settle in. He agreed. We continued up Liberty Street and when we got the corner, we stopped and refueled at the tanker truck that had been placed there for that very purpose.

After I refueled, I drove to the tunnel that led to the FDR Drive. As I moved toward the tunnel, I stopped the truck at the entrance and said to Captain Bentley, "Is it safe to go in there?"

He said, "I think so, are you okay?"

"Yes, just a little nervous after what we have just been through"

"Go slowly, we'll be alright." I moved ever so cautiously into the tunnel, and Chief Wensley commented that he would like to get home sometime that day. I laughed, hit the accelerator, and away we went.

We emerged from the tunnel unscathed and headed past the staging area under the Manhattan Bridge and saw all the replacements getting ready to go into Ground Zero. These people have no idea what they're getting themselves into, I thought. Just as I hadn't known when I was waiting, parked under the Manhattan Bridge.

Exhaustion was starting to set in, and I think Captain Bentley noticed He asked me if I wanted someone else to drive. "I drove us here and I'll drive us home," I responded. He just shook his head and gave me his all too familiar grin.

We got onto the FDR Drive and we were on our way home. My thoughts turned to my wife Dorothy and my children, Brendan and Christian. Again, my eyes welled up and I looked over and saw Dave was probably feeling the same about his family. I got the truck up to speed and said to Captain Bentley, "This truck rides great, doesn't it?" There was that grin again.

I exited the FDR Drive onto First Avenue and when I stopped at the light, we got cheers and waves from everyone in sight. What a great feeling to be appreciated. This is why I'm a firefighter.

I maneuvered my way through the streets of midtown Manhattan towards 34th Street and the entrance to the Midtown Tunnel. When we approached the entrance to the tunnel, we were stopped by a National Guardsman, and he asked where we were going. I thought this somewhat odd, but Captain Bentley explained to them that we had just left Ground Zero and were headed home. The National Guardsman stepped off the side board of the truck, saluted us, and waved us through. The goose bumps started making me realize the enormity of what we had just accomplished although we found no survivors. I'd never worked so hard at anything in my life.

When we entered the Midtown Tunnel, I again felt nervous. I had been in so many voids and holes those forty-eight hours that this big tunnel had me thinking about what could happen once we were inside. I thought, What happens if there is another attack and the tunnel is bombed? These and many other questions would begin to envelop my thoughts

Halfway though the tunnel, I started joking with everyone about who was going to pay the toll on the other end. Everyone roared, and Charlie McEneaney told me to send the bill to Bill Glacken, the Freeport Mayor.

When we reached the end of the tunnel, I could see the

slowdown about five hundred feet before we got out. Again the National Guard was there asking questions. When I pulled the truck up to them, another Guardsman stepped onto the side board of the truck and I asked, "Are you paying the toll?" He laughed with approval, waved us right through, and we were on the Long Island Expressway (L.I.E.) going home to Freeport. It was early Sunday morning and there was no traffic. I yelled to the guys in the back, "Take a look boys, you'll never see this again."

"See what?" Chief Wensley asked.

"See that there is no traffic on the L.I.E.," I explained.

Everyone laughed, but they all looked out the front window of the truck and saw there was no one on the road. I got the truck up to speed and we cruised along at sixty-five miles per hour. Traffic in the west bound direction was a little heavier than east bound as we were going. We still had our lights on and everyone we passed on the opposite direction waved to us and blasted their horns with approval. I was simply too tired to show my appreciation.

At a point about eight miles from Manhattan, I looked in the rear view mirror and saw a column of smoke coming from Ground Zero. I almost cried because even though I was miles from Ground Zero, I could see the smoke with my eyes, feel the soot on my skin, and smell the smoke with my nose. That smell will live with me forever.

We continued along the L.I.E. to the Northern State Parkway to the Meadowbrook Parkway, which led to Freeport. My adrenalin started up again once I got on the Meadowbrook Parkway because I knew it wouldn't be long until I was back in Freeport. I exited onto Sunrise Highway westbound, and we were almost home.

When I drove onto Sunrise Highway, I looked around and genuinely appreciated Freeport. I looked to the left and saw the Freeport Recreation Center and thought how great a swim might be. I was a member of the Aquatic Center at

Eisenhower Park and I would soon be going into the Jacuzzi whirlpool there. Suddenly, I thought of Michael Keifer . . .

~~

I first met Mike Kiefer shortly after he joined Engine Company of the Freeport Fire Department. He was extremely well mannered and always had a smile on his face. I was washing my truck on the ramp of the firehouse one beautiful spring day in 1996 when Mike walked up to me and made small talk. He asked me if I was looking for any help in my construction business.

I told him that I was, and he told me he had a friend, Vinnie Caviello. who was looking for a job. He went on to tell me that Vinnie had some experience and that he was a great guy. He was also a firefighter with the Malverne Fire Department. I told him to have Vinnie call me. He said he would talk to Vinnie that night, and thanked me.

Two days later, Vinnie called, and I told him to come over, and we would talk. I hired him immediately. Vinnie was, and still is very likeable. He worked for me for one year off and on. He was attending school in Oswego, NY and worked when he was home. During the second summer, I was very busy and needed more help.

Vinnie told me that Mike would work if I needed him, so I told Vinnie to bring Mike with him the next day. They both showed up at 8 a.m. and worked for the rest of the summer

Mike was a lifeguard at Jones Beach and worked when he was off. Most of the time we made small talk, and I remember Mike always wanted to be an FDNY firefighter. It was all he talked about. It was part of his very being. He talked about going to fires in Malverne with Vinnie, and how he couldn't wait until he was old enough to be a firefighter. He was consumed with the entire concept of being a firefighter. He made me feel much younger than I was through his energy and his love for the fire service.

Mike finished the summer with me and then moved onto

other jobs. He was young and could afford to move around. I was often jealous of his enthusiasm.

During the next few years, I saw less and less of Mike and Vinnie. Vinnie got a job with a sanitation company, and Mike became an Emergency Medical Technician. In 2000, Mike was hired by the FDNY as an EMT. He worked on an ambulance in New York City. He finally realized his dream when he was hired as a firefighter later that year, and I was happy for him.

During the previous year, I had often seen Mike swimming at the Aquatic Center in Eisenhower Park. He always kept himself in great physical condition, and he always went out of his way to say hello to me. We talked about the FDNY and his being a firefighter.

I remember the day he told me he was hired. He was like a kid with a new toy. He was happy, laughing, and his ever present grin was ear to ear. I saw Mike every time I went to the pool, and he never ceased to amaze me with his positive attitude. He was truly happy.

The last time I saw Mike was on September 2, 2001 at the Aquatic Center. He was swimming his usual laps and when he saw me, he got out of the pool, came right up to me, and told me he was in Ladder 132. Then he said, "Thanks for being my friend."

Mike died in the WTC attack. He was one of a kind, and I will miss him dearly. The entire world will miss him . . .

~~

I gripped the wheel and continued my drive on Sunrise Highway westbound and made a left onto Henry Street at the Dunkin Donuts. I went under the Long Island Railroad tracks, looked up to the left, and saw the firehouse. We were finally home. It was a wonderful sight. I pulled the truck onto the ramp and backed it up.

While driving home from Ground Zero, I'd had many

thoughts about my home town, the Incorporated Village of Freeport. I was born in Freeport Hospital on August 27, 1954 at 11 a.m. Freeport Hospital is now closed as a hospital and the property is going to be redeveloped. I thought about my grandmother, Hazel Smith-Wright, and the fact that she is one of the original Smiths in Freeport. Freeport was once called Raynortown, named after the Raynor family, of which I am a direct descendant. I remembered my grandfather, George Wright, and all the times we sat at his house and he told me stories about his youth. I remember looking at pictures of my father and grandfather at the bay house with my uncle Tiny. I thought about eating lunch at Kelly's bar during the week and marveled at how some people could put away huge amounts of beer. I thought about my children and about Meaghan, my "adopted" daughter, whose heart is in Freeport even though she now lives in California. And finally, I thought long and hard about how I was a legitimate legacy in the Village of Freeport due to my family heritage. I am proud to be a lifelong Freeporter. I hope I made my descendants and my neighbors proud.

Thirteen

# Little League

THE sun was rising in the east at around 6:30 a.m. and careening off what was left of the World Trade Center. It was dulled by the layers of thick dust and soot that covered everything within miles of Ground Zero. Somehow we managed to find all of our equipment with the exception of one pair of bolt cutters.

We knew when we returned to Freeport we would have our work cut out for us in regards to cleaning the truck and all the tools and equipment. Everything was encrusted with dust and soot from the fires at Ground Zero, every nook and cranny. Just before I boarded the truck for the drive home, I saw a pile of crumbled debris about fifty feet from the front of the heavy rescue truck. I stared at it for a while, then I walked up the pile and started pulling it apart and found what was left of a baseball bat. It was only the handle and maybe six inches, but clearly written on the handle was the word Louisville. Anyone who follows baseball knows that Louisville is the home of the manufacturer of the famous Louisville Slugger baseball bats. I bent over, picked it up, and flashed back to my son Christian's Little League playoff game at Glacken Park in Freeport next to the Long Island Railroad tracks . . .

~~

Christian was slated to play second base for this first playoff game on May 17, 2001 against Raimo's Pizza. My wife

Dorothy always takes Christian to the games early for warm-ups and I usually follow about an hour later after I'm finished with business for the day. May 17th was a beautiful spring night, a baseball fan's fantasy. Other parents arrived ahead of me, and I sat down next to Dorothy, who had strategically placed a blanket on the aluminum bleacher seats. Depending on the temperature, the seats were either too hot or too cold to sit on.

Coach Chris was running the team this night and he had his lineup set. Christian was playing second base, and his friend, Davan Garcia was playing shortstop, a true double play tandem. Davan's mother Debbie and brother Dylan were sitting in the stands next to us, and his father Dave was one of the coaches. Dave threw batting practice and coached first base. I first met Dave at Little League tryouts at Atkinson School and was amazed at how adept and knowledgeable at baseball he was. Davan and Dylan, both spitting images of their father, will probably become great baseball players.

The game was about to start, and we cheered our children on with reckless abandon. My wife loves to cheer the team on, almost to frenzy. Just then, the ever-present ice cream truck showed up with its music playing and threw pandemonium into the little league game. Most of the kids asked their parents for money for ice cream. Christian was no different. After a ten-minute delay, the game started. For me, it produced a laugh. Only in America can America's favorite national pastime be subject to the marketing overtures of the local ice cream truck, with the ice cream truck winning every time. God, I love this country.

Coach Chris had become somewhat annoyed at the delay and started his usual yelling at the kids to get the game going. Coach Chris meant well, but yelling at the kids all the time produced little results. When he did give praise, which was not very often, the kids often ignored it. It seems his praise had become like a devalued currency. No one wanted it.

In any case, the game began, went the full required six innings, and we lost. The end of another season was here and most kids just wanted to go eat. Christian and I headed home so he could shower, and Dorothy went to Wendy's to get supper.

When she got home, I had the table ready and Christian had just come out of the shower. We ate dinner then Dorothy and I went for our nightly walk. We talked about how much Christian had improved during the year. I agreed with her and she said, "Can Christian go to baseball camp?"

"That's a great idea" Brendan had attended, and loved the experience.

"I'll look into it tomorrow," she stated.

I went to work the next day. I was working on a window job in North Bellmore when my phone rang. It was Dorothy and she told me that there was a baseball camp in Freeport during the upcoming fall on Sunday mornings at Freeport High School. She also said she was going to make some phone calls to find out the particulars. Within three weeks, Christian was signed up for baseball pitcher's camp. He was so excited when we told him that he couldn't sleep that night. He must have come into my bedroom five or six times during the night. Camp was set to start the third week of September, 2001 and continue for eight consecutive Sundays.

The rest of the summer continued as normal. We went up to my in-laws house in Newfield, New York for a visit. They live in a log cabin on a remote area with no cable television. This is great for adults but questionable for kids. We had a great time when we got there, and then we went to my wife's family reunion in Mansfield, Pennsylvania. We met with all of her family and had a wonderful time talking, playing horseshoes, and swimming. We ended the day with our relatives and drove back to Roger and Janet's house in Newfield. Christian was getting excited because school was starting soon, and then baseball camp would follow. He wore his little league shirt and hat proudly when we were upstate.

After a restful three days, we headed home and with baseball camp on the horizon, it was the only thing Christian would talk about. When we got home, there was a message on my answering machine from the head of the baseball camp. He said there were many other kids from Christian's little league team who were also attending, and that Davan Garcia was one of them. Christian was ecstatic about Davan being at camp. Again, it was all he talked about.

On the Sunday after Labor Day, we had our annual backyard party. Our backyard party had become a tradition since we moved into our house. The tradition began in 1995 when we had about eight friends and relatives over. The event has grown yearly, and on September 9, 2001, just two days before the attacks, we had over seventy people and several fire trucks in attendance. It was controlled mayhem inside and out of the house with kids and adults alike having a blast. No one imagined what was to come two days later.

On September 4, the kids had gone back to school and the third week of September came quickly for Christian. On Sunday mornings, I would drop Christian off at Freeport High School at 8 a.m. for camp and pick him up at 9:30 a.m. Then it was off to church. This went on for several weeks and on the fourth Sunday in October, it was business as usual.

The attacks on the World Trade Center had already occurred and I happened to be home on this particular Sunday. I had already been to Ground Zero for a considerable time, and Dorothy decided to go with me to get Christian. We got there early and walked around for a few minutes until Dorothy saw Debbie Garcia across the room.

I stood there watching Christian practicing in the gym. When I looked across the room, I saw Dorothy and Debbie embracing each other. I thought this was somewhat unusual, but I didn't think about it again. Dorothy had a look of resignation on her face, like the wind had been taken out of her sails.

Practice ended and I walked outside to the car with Christian. We got in, I started the car and waited for Dorothy. She walked over to the car, knocked on the window and asked me to get out. She quickly walked away, so I followed her. "What's wrong Deeej?"

"I don't know how to tell you this."

"Tell me what?"

Dorothy turned to me with tears in her beautiful blue eyes, crackling in her voice, her hands welded to mine and said to me, "Dave was on the ninety-seventh floor of the World Trade Center Tower 1 when it collapsed." She held on to me so tight, it almost took my breath away. My heart raced, I was breathing heavily, and I broke into a cold sweat.

I said, "If he was on the ninety-seventh floor, then there is nothing left. He's gone." My voice crackled. "Get yourself together; we have to tell Christian when we get home."

Somehow we calmed down right away, wiped our eyes and headed for the car. As I opened the car door to get in, I glanced over to Debbie. When she looked at me, I got chills up and down my spine. I didn't know what to say so I said nothing.

I knew Dave Garcia worked for a couple of years for the insurance company Marsh McClennan. I also remember a conversation I'd had with him when we first met. He told me he took either the 7:31 or 7:41 a.m. train into Manhattan and then to the World Trade Center. I told him I used to work for New York City EMS, and that I was often detailed over to lower Manhattan near the trade center.

While we were driving home, Christian sensed something was wrong and asked. I told him I would tell him when we got home. It was only a five minute drive home, but it was the longest five minutes of my life. I kept thinking to myself how I was going to tell Christian that his coach was dead. Every time I thought of it, I felt like I had a brick in my throat. How could I tell him he would never see Coach Dave ever again?

This was going to be extremely difficult but I knew he had to hear it from me. I pulled the car into the driveway and when we got out of the car, I told Dorothy that Christian and I were going for a walk. Dorothy didn't say a word and walked into the house holding her head in her hands, her body making involuntary shakes trying not to cry.

Christian and I walked south on St. Marks Avenue and made a left on Lewis street. When we got to Westside Avenue, I stopped on the corner and we sat down at the curb. I turned to Christian and said, "Chris, I have some bad news for you."

He looked at me with tears in his eyes. "Tell me," he said in a frightened voice, "What's wrong with Mrs. Garcia?"

I touched his shoulder, my eyes tearing, my heart pounding, and said, "Christian, do you remember Coach Dave, Davan and Dylan's Daddy?"

"Yes Daddy, what about him, where is he?" I held his head steady in my hands and answered," Coach Dave was on the ninety-seventh floor of the World Trade Center when it collapsed."

With his eight year old eyes wide with fear, he asked, "Where is he? Is he alright?"

My stomach in knots, my fists clenched, I took a deep breath, turned to Christian and said, "Christian, Coach Dave was in building when it collapsed, and he was killed when he was buried in the rubble."

He stood up, holding his head and said, "You're lying, God would never let that happen to Coach Dave, you're lying."

I stood up, grabbed him by the shoulders, made him

look at me and said, "I'm sorry Christian, but it's true. Davan and Dylan's daddy is dead and there is nothing any of us can do about it now." He screamed out, "No, you're lying. Let's go see him."

"Christian, do you think I would lie about something like this?"

Then he held onto me for dear life and cried uncontrollably. I had to carry him home two blocks to the house, the whole time both of us racked with tears.

When we got into the house, I sat us both on the recliner, and we continued crying. I was devastated that I had to tell my son his Little League coach had been killed in the terrorist attacks. We both cried off and on for about three hours. Dorothy kneeled over and cried along with us. This was the worst day of my life.

That night my nightmares started. The worst was yet to come.

I watched Christian and Davan play ball and marveled at how they had both improved since the beginning of camp. I wondered what went through Davan's mind every time he thought of his father. How did he concentrate? He is a testament to the kind of man his father was.

The next few months flowed like water down a flooded street. After baseball ended, Christian kept asking about Coach Dave. Every time he asked, he cried, I told him how lucky he was that he still had his daddy, and he felt better. I think this is when he started to realize how dangerous it was for me to be working at Ground Zero.

Dorothy and I would drive past the Garcia house once in a while, say hello, and ask if we could help in any way. Christian would always play with Davan and Dylan. On one occasion, Jimmy Butler, who is one of the Freeport Fire Chiefs, and also lived next door to the Garcia's, was in his driveway so I struck up a conversation with him.

We reminisced about when we were kids and when we used to take newspapers to the recycling center on Merrick Road and cash them in for money. Jimmy lived around the corner from me with his family. Everyone always thought Jimmy was older because he's taller than most. We didn't talk about Dave Garcia. It seemed as though it was taboo.

Jimmy and I finished our conversation when Dorothy and Christian walked down Debbie Garcia's driveway. Dorothy, Christian and I got in the car and drove home.

~~

We had been at Ground Zero for about six hours, and I had come down off the pile to get a drink. When you came down off the pile, you never really rested because there was always so much to do. While I stood there drinking water, I suddenly got bumped into by one of the FDNY firefighters. I was almost knocked over when I turned and there was Jimmy Butler. Jimmy has been a FDNY firefighter for a long time and when he purposely bumped me, I was glad to see him.

I had been handing up buckets to the top of one of the bucket brigades when he showed up. We stood there for a while and talked about how destructive this was, the entire time standing side by side handing up buckets. I've known him for my entire life, but somehow now I felt connected to him like never before. The pain etched on his face was unmistakable.

After about twenty minutes of bucket brigade, I was called back to the pile for another assignment. Chief Wensley waved Jimmy over to him and when I climbed back up the pile, I looked back and saw them watching me. Jimmy yelled out in his sarcastic voice, "Be careful rookie, this climbing stuff in new to you." I laughed and continued on up. When I reached my Freeport brothers, I looked back, Jimmy was gone, and John Wensley just shook his head smiling.

I was now on my hands and knees digging, and I couldn't stop thinking about all the Freeport people who were here working at this arduous task. I had seen Jimmy Butler, Julie Ellison, Rob Middleton, Frank Fee, Paul Hashagan, Mike Sotira, Kevin Muldowney, Freeport Police Officer Rich Samuels, along with my Freeport Rescue brothers at Ground Zero. I have come to realize that in spite of our differences over the years, none of that mattered anymore. We were all there for the same reason, doing the same thing, trying to rescue our brothers and make some sense out of all this. But there would never be a way to make sense of this.

Fifteen
# Home Sweet Home

LT. Bill McBride showed up at the firehouse to help with
the clean up detail just as we left the company quarters to go
outside. He must have sensed I was angry over something
that Chief John Maguire had just said to us upon our return
from Ground Zero. I followed Chief Maguire outside to give
him a piece of my mind when Bill grabbed my arm, turned
me around and said, "Jonny boy, where are you going?"

I refrained from cursing, but thought to myself that
Chief Maguire could use some help refining his people skills.
Lt. McBride strongly suggested I not cause a fracas, then
ordered me to the back room of the firehouse to discuss the
situation.

When we arrived in the back room, Lt. McBride
questioned me as to what had happened. I repeated to him
how upset I was with the chief and what I wanted to do
about it.

We sat down, and he suggested a long, deep breath. I
could sense how red my face was and feel the vein popping
from the left side of my neck. Truly a discomforting feeling.

I described how John Maguire had come into company
quarters after Chief Russer had requested we all go inside —
before starting our truck cleaning detail. Maguire suggested
there were other volunteers who should have gone to
Ground Zero before us.

Chief Russer, on the other hand, had made it clear that
he knew we had just been to hell and back, and that some of

us would begin to experience emotional turmoil. Given the circumstances and the fact that we were all exhausted, his comments were welcome and appreciated, as was his candor.

After I explained to Lt. McBride what had transpired, he laughed and said, "He really pushed you button, didn't he?"

"He really doesn't know how lucky he is," I responded.

"Probably not," Bill said.

We walked back into the living room where the others had congregated and were talking about what the chief had said. They seemed concerned that I was going to do something stupid. I assured them that I was calmed down, and we all went outside and started working on the truck. Luckily for him, John Maguire was gone.

I grabbed the hose and started hosing down the outside of the truck. When the water careened off the red paint, it looked like mud puddles forming at the base of the truck. It was gray in color and smelled like Ground Zero. That smell will be with me for the rest of my life. It is seared into my memory. I put my hand into one of the piles that had formed, and the gray stuff was like paste. It was everywhere.

After we washed the outside, I turned the truck around. Lt. Tucker and Charlie McEneaney opened the rear door and pulled out the plastic mats that lined the floor. Charlie Manning lined them up against the building and rinsed them off. When he went to put them back, the red brick wall of the firehouse had this gray paste all over it in the outline of the plastic mats, as did the floor inside the back of the truck.

The soot and dust had encapsulated the inside of the truck as well. We had to empty each and every compartment on the truck, inside and out. There was not a single place where the soot and dust had not gotten into. To this day, I can still taste it. True to his word, Chief Russer was cleaning the truck along with us. I personally applauded his effort and thanked him for his help.

We cleaned continually for about two hours. We had to

put the truck back in service for two reasons. First, if there was a call, we had to be able to respond. Second, and equally important, if we were summoned to respond back to Ground Zero, we had to be ready at a moments notice. When I left the firehouse, the truck was in tip top condition, although some of us went back and washed it again that night. I went up to each of my brothers and thanked them for being there with me. Chief Wensley, Captain Bentley, Lt. Tucker, Charlie McEneaney, and Charlie Manning each brought me new meaning to the word brotherhood, and I love them for it.

Finally, I sat down on a chair that someone brought out from the firehouse. I decided it was time to take off the boots that the support services personnel had given me. God did that feel good to get them off. I sat on the ramp of the firehouse and ran the hose on my feet for about ten minutes. It was pure ecstasy.

Wanting to get home to my family, I sauntered over to my truck, opened the back door and put my fire gear inside. I walked gingerly to the driver seat and used all my strength to climb in. I was so tired my eyes watered. I wiped them with a paper towel and started the ten-minute drive home.

I decided to stop at Bob's Luncheonette and get the Sunday papers. I walked in and a couple of my firefighting friends were at the big round table. They waved and smiled. They knew what I had just been through and by the expression in their eyes, I could tell they appreciated what I had just done with my rescue brothers. I paid for the papers and walked back out to my truck, got in and drove home. It was a beautiful Sunday morning with blue skies, low humidity, and fresh air. What more could a man ask for. I pulled onto St. Marks Avenue and backed my truck into my driveway.

I put it in park, opened the door, and stepped out. Just as I walked to the back of the truck to get my gear, my son Christian, who was still in his pajamas, swung the front door to the house open and screamed out, "Mommy, Daddy's home." He ran at full speed about twenty feet and jumped into my arms. He hugged and kissed me and said, "Are you all right, Daddy?"

"I am now," I said softly, and felt a renewed sense of sanctuary. He held onto me for dear life as my wife Dorothy came walking out to greet me. She walked up to me, looked at me with her baby blues and said nothing. When she looked into my eyes, she knew how bad it really was. She realized at that exact moment how dangerous and afraid I had been. She kissed me, hugged me, and kissed me again. Then I cried. It felt incredibly good to be home, be alive, and be with my family.

We walked in the house and I melted into my recliner. Christian sat on my lap like a lap dog and kept hugging me. Dorothy kneeled down next to us and gently massaged my shoulders and neck. I was exhausted so it didn't take long for me to almost fall asleep. I told her, "Honey, I'm going upstairs to take a shower and go to bed."

Knowing I liked my feet massaged, she said, "When you come out, I'll rub your feet."

" You've got a deal."

I took a shower and went into the bedroom to lie down. She heard the bedroom door close from downstairs and she came up to rub my feet. Before she started she asked, "Do you want to go to church with us?"

"No, you go, and say a prayer for all of us?"

She rubbed my feet and I must have fallen asleep within two minutes because I don't remember her leaving the room. It was 10 a.m. I woke at 12 noon refreshed and ready to tackle the world. I went downstairs and Dorothy asked, "What are you doing up?"

" I can't sleep. I don't know why, but I can't sleep."

"When are you going back to Ground Zero?"

"Probably tonight or tomorrow."

Then she asked, "When are you going to the firehouse?"

"What makes you think I'm going to the firehouse?"

She looked at me with her gorgeous baby blue eyes and said, "You're kidding, right?"

I just smiled and said, "You think you know me, huh."

She answered, "Yup."

I said nothing and went upstairs to get dressed. Christian followed and asked, "Daddy, are you going back to Ground Zero?"

I saw fear and tears in his eyes. I knew I had to be very careful with my response so I said, "Christian, if they need me and call me to go back and try to rescue people, I have to go. God would want me to."

He held on to me again and started crying, which started me crying. I knew I had to go, but I also knew I had a family. Most important, I knew if I didn't go back, I would never forgive myself. Then I said, "Christian, right now I am too tired to even think about it."

He asked, "Daddy, can I go to the firehouse with you?"

"You're worse than you mother. Of course you can."

I finished dressing and went back downstairs, told Dorothy we would be back in a couple of hours, and went out to the front porch where my turnout gear was. I looked and realized I had to clean it. I got out the garden hose and rinsed it off.

When I finished, there was a puddle of gray mud from all the dust and soot on my driveway. I also took the piece of steel beam out of my turnout pants pocket. This was the piece that had to be cut off the woman with the steel reinforcement rod penetrating her torso. I stopped dead still and started crying and shaking. Christian ran inside and got Dorothy. She saw me crying and ran up to me and held me. She asked, "What's wrong honey?"

"We had to cut this piece off this woman so we could take out her body from inside the pile. I'm sorry for crying."

She didn't say a word, but she held me tight. That's when I knew eventually everything was going to be okay. Her embrace was the most reassuring thing that had happened in the past four days. It felt breathtaking. She held my face and said, "Go to the firehouse and take care of business, but you come home for dinner."

I told her I would be home by 5 p.m.

I left for the firehouse at 12:30 p.m. and arrived five minutes later. When I got there, Captain Bentley, Lts. McBride and Tucker, and Charlie Manning were already there working on the truck, preparing for our return to Ground Zero. Lt. McBride looked at me, grinned, and said, "What took you so long? I hope you didn't go home to sleep at all."

I laughed and quipped, "I just thought I would leave the work for all you rookies."

Captain Bentley interjected, "Let's go dinosaur, we have work to do. Stop yapping and get to work."

Everyone laughed as I opened the Hurst Tool compartment. Inside the compartment are two drawers that house the different tools and attachments for the Hurst Tool. I pulled on the top drawer and opened it. Inside I found a couple of pieces from Ground Zero that I had put inside just before we departed. Included in the pieces were some small chunks of pulverized concrete – the most significant the four foot piece of mangled steel reinforcement rod – part of the rod that was cut off the woman we found with the rest of the rod piercing her body.

Again I stopped, looked at the rod, and corralled every ounce of my strength to sustain my self-control. With a knot in my stomach and my heart pounding, I took the piece and walked inside with it. I placed it on the floor and when I turned, Lt. McBride was standing there and he asked, "Are you all right?"

I said, "Did it show that much?"

"More than you want to know. Everyone saw the look

on your face."

"I didn't fool anyone, did I?"

" Nope."

He put his hands on my arms and reassured me by saying, "It's going to be okay."

"I know," I said, and walked out the door to the apparatus floor. I walked back to the Hurst Tool compartment and started removing everything inside. When I got everything out, I looked at the sliding tray and there was a layer of dust on it that we missed when we cleaned the truck after our arrival back home. I grabbed some towels and wiped the drawers and when I finished, the towels were dark gray in color and had to be thrown out.

After I finished wiping the tools off, I started on the hoses that supply hydraulic fluid to the tool during its operation. I pulled four-hundred feet of hose off and started wiping it also with towels, and when I finished, I had to throw them out as well. The soot and gray dust were everywhere. Everything we touched had this stuff on it. Nothing was exempt. I thought we'd made a big dent in the work to be done on the truck, but I was wrong. It took another four hours to make the truck presentable. We worked relentlessly to get everything back to normal. When we finished, we went inside, sat the bar, and tried to have a conversation. No one seemed willing to talk. We sat there silent. Numb.

Finally, I yelled out, "How about them Jets?"

That brought about a small chuckle and seemed to break the ice. Charlie McEneany had come in and true to form, told a joke, which made everyone laugh. We finally were able to converse, but only on a very low emotional level. Clearly we were not ourselves, but we knew we could depend on each other.

I made my goodbyes and left for home. I was uncomfortable sitting there unable to talk about what we had just been through. In retrospect, I think the sight of the steel reinforcement rod and pulverized concrete in the Hurst Tool drawer and subsequently inside the firehouse, made us all increasingly in tune with the severity of our own emotional trauma. I think we all felt the same way. When I returned home, Dorothy and Christian again met me at the front porch. I walked up and sat on my favorite chair. Christian sat on my lap. We made small talk and I told Dorothy about all the work we had just finished.

I told her the truck was finally ready to go back and she said, "When are you going back?"

"Just as soon as I can."

She walked inside the house and got a menu from our favorite Chinese take out. I knew she was upset that I was going back to Ground Zero, but I also knew she understood why I had to go when called. We ordered and she went to pick it up. Christian and I sat on the porch until her return. While she was gone, I missed her like she had been gone for three months. Probably because I felt so vulnerable, I think. When she returned, I walked up to the car, opened the door, and hugged her when she got out.

We ate dinner and sat on the front porch when Christian came from the back yard with two lacrosse sticks and asked if we could have a catch. I blurted out, "Absolutely."

We started playing catch and I flashed back to 1972 during one of my high school lacrosse games . . .

~~

This was the last game of the regular season and we had to win to make the playoffs. We were playing Seawanaka High School from Elmont, NY and needed this win. Seawanaka was the dominant team from Long Island and we knew it was going to be a tough game. I wasn't a starter but I played defense in man down situations. My defense partners were John Pastore and Joe "Bubba" Falco. Bubba was an exceptional defenseman as was John, but I was average, nothing more. I felt very lucky to be playing in such an important game.

The game started and within minutes, we had a penalty. Attack man Kevin Pierce had been called for slashing, so on the field I went. Seawanaka brought the ball into the offensive zone a passed the ball at will. We were moving and protecting our goalie when one of the Seawanaka players came across the crease with the ball.

He went to take a shot and Bubba flattened him. He never even got his shot off. He lost the ball; I picked it up and ran to midfield. I passed off the ball to one of our midfielders who ran to the other end as I returned to the defensive end. The Seawanaka player was very slow getting up and when I looked at Bubba, he was smiling. We were all smiling. Although they didn't score during the penalty, they did win the game and bumped us out of the playoffs and officially, my high school lacrosse career was over. Bubba and John still had one year to play, but I was a senior. My playing days finished . . .

~~

We had played catch for about half an hour when I told Christian I was tired and wanted to stop. He asked me to keep going, but I was too tired. I sat down on the porch and he sat next to me. Christian asked, "Daddy, do you ever see any of the guys you played lacrosse with in high school?"

"Yes I do. In fact, I took one of the guys who got hurt at Ground Zero to a specialist on Wednesday." He asked, "Who was that, Daddy?"

"His name is Bubba." ...

~~

I flashed back to September 12th. I'd been at the firehouse the better part of the day. I had also gone back to the job and checked with my customer Jack, who made it crystal clear it was okay that I wasn't there.

At 12 noon, I was up in the chief's office with Chief

Wensley waiting on word of our fallen brethren. We already knew about the five firefighters who were missing, and we talked about those firefighters from Freeport that we could not account for.

I knew Bruce Newbery, Paul Hashagan, and Frank Fee were in Freeport at the time of the attacks. I knew Jackie Collins, who had recently retired, was out at the bay house. I knew John Fee was home because he lives around the corner from me. No one knew where Bubba was.

Chief Wensley told me the guys from Truck company didn't know where he was either. He was due to get off duty. but no one could account for him.

With everyone who had been confirmed lost, I was barraged with emotional uncertainty. I've known Bubba for almost my entire life and I was really worried about his well-being. My heart began to sink. I went back down to the apparatus floor and continued preparing the truck for anything that could arise. We had received faxes about more terrorist activity, so I made it my personal business to make sure all was well with the heavy rescue truck. Every infinitesimal detail was checked and rechecked.

At 4 p.m., I was inside the company quarters when the phone rang. It was Captain Bentley. "Bubba is alive."

I asked, "Where is he?"

"He was in the traffic circle in front of the trade center when it collapses and ran for his life." Captain Bentley added, "When he ran down the street, he fell and destroyed his knee."

I asked, "Where is he now?"

" He was taken by ferry to New Jersey, then by bus back to Manhattan, then home. The chief wants to know if we can take him to the orthopedist tomorrow."

"Count me in," I said.

I continued preparing the heavy rescue truck and then I operated each and every piece of equipment on the truck to make certain it was working properly. I went home at 5:30 p.m. and met Dorothy there. She had left work early that day, picked up Christian from school and gone home. When I got there, they met me at the front door and the first thing she said was, "Are you going to Ground Zero?"

I answered, "Yes, if they call me."

That was the first time I ever saw fear in Dorothy's eyes. She said nothing, went into the kitchen, and made dinner. A few minutes later, I looked in the kitchen and saw she had been crying. Christian was outside playing with Victor from across the street. I went into the kitchen and reassured Dorothy that I would be all right, even though I knew I would be going into the collapse zone. I couldn't show her any fear because that would have made things worse. I assured her that I would be okay.

Little did I know I would break my left wrist that night. We had dinner and after I kissed Dorothy and Christian, I returned to the firehouse. When I got there, a crowd had already gathered to see what, if anything could be done. Everyone kept busy doing something, but I watched CNN on television. At 8 p.m. Captain Bentley told me we would be taking Bubba to the doctor at 11 a.m. the next morning. I told him I would meet him there at 10. I had also told Chief Wensley that I would be keeping the fire department EMS car until further notice.

I took the car home each night and kept it at work during the day. I had the car 24/7. After speaking with the chief, Captain Bentley decided that the car should be in service full time until after the crisis passed. I was the most experienced firefighter in the department with advanced medical training, and my experience and decisions could be critical in certain situations. It was a smart and logical move. Captain Bentley had already made the decisions about the fly car.

I went back home on September 12th at 11 p.m. The

next morning I woke up at 6 a.m. and immediately headed for the firehouse. When I got there, I found several members had slept there all night to make sure we had a crew in case of a call. Charlie McEneany was watching television when I walked in, and he asked, "Are you going on the transport?"

"Yes I am. I'll have the fly car, but I am going to stay in service at all times." I added, "Bubba has been my friend for over thirty years and I owe it to him to help."

We watched television and every time they replayed the attacks, my stomach churned, my mind raced, and anger started to rear its ugly head. After a while, I asked if anyone wanted breakfast. We called and ordered from the deli, but they would have taken an hour to deliver. Charlie and I made a McDonald's run and returned to the firehouse with breakfast within fifteen minutes.

By the time we returned Captain Bentley and Firefighter Kevin McKeown had arrived to assist with the transport. Unbeknownst to me, Kevin had moved into the house right next door to Bubba. He told us that Bubba looked terrible and that he was in considerable pain. He went on to tell is that getting Bubba out of his house was going to be a difficult task. Bubba only stands about five feet five inches tall, but is solid as a rock. He is short in stature but has the heart and soul of a lion. He is truly one of the nice guys and I am honored to call him friend.

We headed to Bubba's house at 10:30 and got there five minutes later. When I walked into his house, his wife Janice met me at the door. She hugged and kissed me and I asked how Bubba's spirits were. She started crying slightly, but managed to compose herself before Bubba saw her. I cannot imagine what she must have thought when she learned the towers collapsed. She is a wonderful friend, terrific wife and great mother. Bubba and her children are indeed lucky to have her.

I asked if he was ready, and she said he was working his

way out of the bathroom. I walked toward the rear of the house and looked to my left and saw him struggling to get into the living room. I went up to him and asked what I could do to help. I had to muster all my internal fortitude to keep myself from losing it emotionally. Bubba looked as though he had been through a twenty round prize-fight.

I walked over to him and put my arm around him and helped him out of the bathroom. I fought back tears when I saw he still had gray dust in his hair, and that was after he had been cleaned up. I helped him through his dining room into his living room where we had the stretcher set up. He hobbled over and lay down on the stretcher by the front door. I was in emotional turmoil but kept my wits about me.

Kevin, Dave, Charlie, and I picked up the stretcher and carried Bubba out to the waiting ambulance and placed him inside. The others loaded up and I got into the fly car just in time for my eyes to tear. It was heartbreaking. Bubba had been a firefighter for over twelve years, and I knew how much he loved his job that was now in jeopardy. I followed the ambulance to Dr. Benatar's office in Bellmore where we unloaded Bubba. When we got inside, the doctor's office was on the fourth floor and the elevators were "Nonoperational" as the sign indicated.

Than meant we had to carry Bubba up four flights to the doctor's office. After what he had been through, I would have carried him twenty flights alone if need be. The four of us carried him up and when we got into the office, the doctor took him right in ahead of everyone else waiting their turns. One person complained about Bubba going in ahead of everyone else, but was quickly put in his place. I was in no mood for nonsense.

While we waited, the others in the waiting room were silent. There was no conversation, no small talk, nothing. Just deafening silence. He emerged from the examination room thirty minutes later and we carried him back down to the waiting ambulance and then home. Once we got him home, the others left. I stayed a while and we talked.

I sat in his living room and he told me he was never so afraid of anything in his life. "I'm not going to die here," he said to himself after the initial building collapse, which sent him literally flying across the West Side Highway. He explained, "It was pitch black after the first collapse and after I was thrown across the divider of the West Side Highway. I just laid there in total darkness, unable to breath, choking from the smoke and dust. It was eerily silent. I kept calling for my partner, Tyrone," he said emphatically.

He continued, "I was crawling in the middle of the West Side Highway looking and feeling for anything when I heard a cry for help. I looked up and saw the headlights of an FDNY ambulance sitting in the middle of the road half covered with collapse debris. The cry for help was coming from underneath the ambulance that was now on fire.

"Just then, three FDNY firefighters walked up and asked if I needed help and I told them I was okay but there was someone under the ambulance. I told them to help them first, I'd be alright."

He went on to explain to me that he had to work his way across the walkway across the West Side Highway in complete darkness. He told me when he got there the staircase going down about ten steps was still intact. With a broken knee and other assorted injuries, he said, "I painstakingly made my way down the steps and started walking straight towards the water. I just kept walking in a straight line. By this time," he explained, "My knee and leg were agonizing, but I knew I had to keep going. When I got to the water by the West Side Highway, I was picked up by a ferry and taken to the Jersey City Medical Center in Jersey City, New Jersey."

He also told me he was about to go off duty when the first plane hit the south tower. "I was driving Engine 1 from

31st Street because my relief hadn't arrived yet. I parked the rig near the north tower right behind Engine 65 and helped the others with their firefighting duties," he said. "I helped the other guy connect to the fire hydrant on the West Side Highway."

Bubba told me his duty Lieutenant was killed along with the Captain of the Truck Company from his firehouse. He said when he got the Jersey City Medical Center, all the cops and firefighters were taken to a separate area away from everyone else to deal with their injuries. After he was treated, he was taken by bus back to Manhattan and picked up by two Freeport firefighters and brought home. Disillusionment covered his face.

~~

Christian and I finished our lacrosse catch and sat on the front porch and had a cold drink that Dorothy had brought out. Later that day, Brendan called from upstate and asked if I was all right. He also asked about Ground Zero and I told him we would talk about it after he came home. After dinner, Christian and I went back to the firehouse and worked on the truck some more. After telling him Bubba's story, Christian decided he was going to play lacrosse in high school and asked Victor from across the street to have a lacrosse catch.

That was extraordinary.

## Sixteen
# To the Front of the Line

SEPTEMBER 11th had come and passed. I've been at Ground Zero more times than I want to admit. It has been tormenting both emotionally and physically. My left wrist throbbed daily and caused me many days of missed work. I actually broke my wrist the first day at Ground Zero. While climbing out of a void backwards, another firefighter from the FDNY slipped and fell on top of me.

I knew my wrist was injured, but in the big picture, it was irrelevant. I'd kept working daily and when I went into Ground Zero, I put the pain completely out of my mind. Chief Wensley pointedly asked if anyone was hurt when we left Ground Zero the first day. I kept my mouth shut for fear it would keep me from going back and searching.

One day towards the end of October, Lt. Tucker and I were preparing the heavy rescue truck for another trip into Ground Zero. He was working on the air bag compartment while I was working on the Hurst Tool compartment. I had taken the portable Hurst Tool generator out of the compartment and was doing the weekly maintenance. I was talking to Lt. Tucker and at the same time trying to start the generator. The Hurst Tool generator has a high compression ratio, which means it is hard to start due to the internal pressure when pulling the rope to start it. I was having trouble starting it. Lt. Tucker said, "Let me try."

"Absolutely not. It is not going to get the best of me." I grabbed the starter and pulled as hard as I could. The internal was so compression high that when I pulled it, it recoiled before I could let go of the starter and it pulled my left wrist back into the generator itself. I immediately dropped to my knees and Lt. Tucker, who had seen it, ran over to me.

He asked, "Are you all right?"

The pain was excruciating and I could barely breathe. I was holding my left wrist in my right hand and he said, "Breathe, Jon."

I was unable to talk; unable to communicate in any way. I sat back up against the building and started breathing again and screamed out, "God Dammit that hurt."

"How bad is it?"

"It's broken."

"Do you want to go to the hospital?"

"No, I'll call my own doctor." He told me to go home and put ice on it.

"Frank, I think I'm finished at Ground Zero," I said.

"Is it that bad?"

"It is definitely broken," I replied.

"How do you know?"

"Frank, I broke my other wrist in 1991. This is exactly what it felt like."

Frank helped me up and inside the firehouse. I put some ice on my wrist and began pacing around. The pain was incredible. It made me nauseous, and the wrist began to swell. It got so bad at one point I had to go into the bathroom and wash my face. After a few minutes I came out and told Frank I was going home.

"Do you want me to call Dorothy?" He said.

"Absolutely not."

I walked out of the firehouse, got into my truck, and headed home. Dorothy wasn't home yet and I was hoping that when she got home, the pain would have subsided enough to let me get on with my life. Fat chance that would happen.

Dorothy got home at 5:30 p.m., walked into the house and kissed me hello. "What's wrong?"

"Nothing," I replied.

She gave me one of her looks. "Bullshit."

Realizing I was fooling no one, I said, "I think I broke my wrist."

"Wonderful."

I went on to explain what happened the first day at Ground Zero and why I had to keep it from everyone, including her. She said nothing and went upstairs to change. When she came down she said, "Did you call Dr. Kamler?

"Yes, it was the first thing I did when I got home."

"When is your appointment?" she asked.

"Tomorrow at 2 p.m.," I answered.

"Good, I'll go with you."

"Not a chance you are going with me."

She laughed and went into the kitchen where she continued laughing. She knew there was no way I would let her come with me to the doctor. Just then, the phone rang. It was Lt. McBride asking how I was.

"How did you know?"

"I know everything," he replied.

I laughed again and explained to him that I originally hurt it the first day at Ground Zero. I also told him I had a doctor's appointment the next day and afterward I would call him and let him know what happened.

He wished me luck and said good-bye.

I went to bed that night in excruciating pain and when I arose the next morning, although my wrist was tender, it didn't hurt as it had the day before. Dorothy had already left for work and just as I was leaving the house, the phone rang and she was on the other end. "Are you going to work today," she asked.

"I'm going to try like hell," I answered.

"Call me as soon as you're done."

I agreed and headed off to work.

I arrived at the job in Baldwin, NY at 9 a.m. This was a good job for me because it gave me the opportunity to rebuild a termite infested back porch. The house was owned by a man named Tom, whose cousin Noreen was a neighbor of mine. I did a similar job for her a couple years prior.

Tom was a retired FDNY firefighter and his son Tom Jr. was a volunteer firefighter in Baldwin.

Jim 'the Dude' Sands, who had been working for me off and on for the past six years, accompanied me to the job. Jim is an interesting man. Jim and Tom talked often about the FDNY and I am always amazed at Jim's knowledge of the FDNY.

Tom was truly moved by the events of September 11 and spoke of his brother firefighters often, at times reducing us to tears. Tom's son was also the firefighter who was photographed sleeping against a building after one of his shifts at Ground Zero. That photo was on the front page of almost every magazine in the country.

I helped Jim set up the scaffolding on the job and quickly realized that I was unable to work due to my fractured wrist. I got him started and called Dr. Ken Kamler, a renowned hand surgeon. Due to the nature and cause of my injury, he reconfirmed my appointment for the next day and told me to come in at 2 p.m.

I went home and called Dorothy and told her what happened and she was very unhappy that I hadn't told her the extent of my injury. She was infuriated that I had gone back to Ground Zero and continued searching for my brothers. To me, giving in to pain was not an option, so I'd put it out of my head.

I iced my wrist for the remainder of the day and it felt markedly better that night, but I still knew it was broken. The next morning I got dressed and went over to the job to see how Jim was doing. He had made good progress, and I was please to find there was no more termite damage than originally thought. Tom was also happy and Jim was able to start closing in the damaged area. We would finish the job by the following Friday.

That afternoon I went to see Dr. Kamler at his office at Long Island Jewish Hospital in New Hyde Park, NY. When I got there I walked in, signed in, and took a seat. My past experience told me I would be there for a couple of hours. However, when I picked up the newspaper to read, I was called into an examination room immediately.

I found this odd, so when they called my name, I questioned the receptionist about why I was taken ahead of all the other people in the waiting room. She motioned me over to the desk and said, "Dr. Kamler told us to take you in as soon as you got here because of the way you hurt your wrist."

I asked, "Are you sure?"

To which she answered, "Absolutely Mr. Wright, just go into exam room #2."

I walked in without turning around because I didn't want to look at all the others who had been forced to wait. I felt guilty about going ahead of the others, but the pain in my wrist was far greater than the question mark on my conscience, so in I went. When Dr. Kamler came into the room, he asked exactly what happened and I told him. He ordered an x-ray on my wrist and left the room until after the x-ray was taken.

When he returned, he looked at the x-ray, turned to me and said, "I have good news and bad news."

"What is the bad news?"

"The bad news is your wrist has a hairline fracture of the hamate bone." He continued, "The good news is you will only be in a cast for six weeks."

I looked at him and said, "You only gave me bad news."

He said, "The cast part was the good news. Remember

when you broke your other wrist, you were in a cast for twelve weeks. This time it is only six weeks."

I laughed and said to him, "Is there any way I can wear a removable brace instead of a cast?"

He retorted," No."

That was when I started begging. I explained to him that if I have a cast on my wrist, there was no way I would be able to work. I went onto tell him if I can't work, I will have no money coming in (not exactly truthful). In any case, he agreed after significant begging. I walked out with a removable splint on my left wrist that I had to wear for eight weeks instead of six. A compromise I could live with.

On the way home, I called Dorothy and told her what Dr. Kamler said. The first words out of her mouth were, "What did he really say?"

Playing dumb, I responded, "What do you mean?"

She angrily said, "I know you better than you think. Now for the last time, what did he say?"

Knowing the jig was up, I told her the whole story and when I finished she said, "I would pay good money to see you grovel."

"Ha Ha Ha," I said in return.

I continued home towards Freeport and went to the firehouse. When I arrived, Lt. Tucker was there working on the heavy rescue truck. I walked up to him and he smiled right away and asked how badly it was broken. I told him what the doctor said and went inside. He followed me inside and asked if there was anything he could do for me. I told him I would be all right. I left the firehouse and went home to heal.

# Epilog

As this book is hitting the book stores, the nation is still in a healing phase. The events of 9/11 are forever burned into our national psyche. Those of us who experienced first hand the horrific tragedy at Ground Zero continue to search for ways to deal with our experiences. Writing this book has helped the process of emotional healing.

My wrist has not completely healed. I still receive medical attention, and have undergone several surgeries. My heart has not healed, either. Perhaps the passing of time will help. Perhaps not.

I've come to love my new method of self-expression. I find there is much to tell about life in the small village of Freeport. If you care to come along with me on my writing journey, please watch for my next book.

*Jonathan Wright*

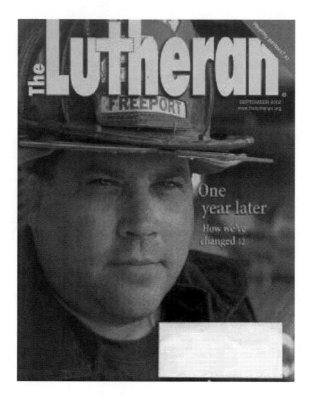

Jon Wright on the cover of the September
2002 issue of THE LUTHERAN magazine.